LUCIEN LÉVY-BRUHL

EXPLORATIONS IN INTERPRETATIVE SOCIOLOGY

GENERAL EDITORS

PHILIP RIEFF

Benjamin Franklin Professor of Sociology
University of Pennsylvania

BRYAN R. WILSON

Reader in Sociology, University of Oxford
Fellow of All Souls College

Also in this series

MAX WEBER AND SOCIOLOGY TODAY
Edited by Otto Stammer
Translated by Kathleen Morris

THE SOCIAL FRAMEWORKS OF KNOWLEDGE
Georges Gurvitch
Translated by M. A. and K. A. Thompson

Forthcoming

THE CARNETS OF LÉVY-BRUHL
Translated by Peter Rivière

FALSE CONSCIOUSNESS
Joseph Gabel
Translated by M. A. and K. A. Thompson

FROM SYMBOLISM TO STRUCTURALISM:
Lévi-Strauss in a Literary Tradition
James A. Boon

LUCIEN LÉVY-BRUHL

By

JEAN CAZENEUVE

Translated by

PETER RIVIÈRE

HARPER & ROW, PUBLISHERS

NEW YORK, EVANSTON, SAN FRANCISCO, LONDON

Printed in Great Britain for Harper & Row, Publishers

For information address Harper & Row, Publishers, Inc.,
49 East 33rd Street, New York, N.Y. 10016

First published in French as
Lucien Lévy-Bruhl, sa vie, son oeuvre
avec un exposé de sa philosophie

and translated by arrangement.

Standard Book Number (Cloth): 06-13-6081-3

Library of Congress Catalog Card Number: 72-75622

CONTENTS

TRANSLATOR'S NOTE

Although many of the works of Lévy-Bruhl have already been published in an English version, the extracts from these works which are included in this volume have been checked and revised. This means that while many of the sentences remain as they appeared in the original translations, others have been changed either partially or completely. My reasons for making these alterations are either because I felt that they failed to convey Lévy-Bruhl's intended meaning or because, through the lapse of time, certain words and expressions needed updating.

A small addition which has been made to this English version is to include the exact references of the extracts of Lévy-Bruhl's works.

I am grateful for advice and assistance from Rodney Needham and Sarah Rivière in the preparation of this translation.

Oxford, 1970 P. R.

BIOGRAPHICAL NOTE

Lucien Lévy-Bruhl, who was born in Paris on 10th April, 1857, of a family which came from Metz, had an exceptionally brilliant school career at the *lycée* Charlemagne. In the competitive examination which takes place each year among the best pupils of the French secondary schools, Gustave Lanson and he divided between them a good part of the prizes. At this time the future sociologist wavered between two careers: that of philosopher and that of orchestral conductor, and he was to show throughout his life a very active interest in music. His intellectual gifts could also have directed him towards l'École polytechnique, but in the end he chose to prepare for the examination in the literary department of l'École normale supérieure which he entered in 1876. Not yielding to the advice of the director, Fustel de Coulanges, who pressed him to become an historian, Lucien Lévy-Bruhl turned towards the *agrégation* in philosophy which, together with his fellow pupil Jean Jaurès, he obtained in 1879. Schooled in this subject by Jules Lachelier, he was also interested in psychopathology and took some clinical courses at Sainte-Anne. On leaving the rue d'Ulm he was first appointed teacher at Poitiers (1879–82) where he used to meet music lovers at the salon of the Countess de La Rochebrochard. Afterwards he taught philosophy at Amiens (1882–3), where he married the daughter of a diamond merchant who was the cousin of the future great mathematician Hadamard. Of this marriage were born three children, the second of whom, Henri (1884), was to become famous in the field of the sociology of law.

Lucien Lévy-Bruhl submitted his doctoral theses in 1884. The principal one was concerned with the idea of responsibility, and the title of the Latin thesis was *Quid de deo Seneca senserit.* Appointed to Paris a year before obtaining his doctorate, Lévy-Bruhl was at first professor of Higher Rhetoric at the *lycée* Louis-le-Grand (1883–95), and then a supplementary lecturer at l'École normale supérieure. In 1896 he was appointed to the Sorbonne, where, having occupied different grades, he became in 1904 titular professor of the history of modern philosophy and director of studies in philosophy. At the same time, he continued to give a course at l'École libre des Sciences politiques, the founder of which, his friend Boutmy, had since 1886 entrusted him with the teaching of the history of political ideas and public opinion in Germany since 1815.

From his arrival at the Sorbonne until 1914, Lévy-Bruhl exercised a profound influence on the students. Large audiences used to throng the Descartes lecture room to get the advantage of the light which he threw on the systems of the great philosophers. He spoke without notes, only occasionally taking from an envelope a card from which he read a quotation. As Péguy wrote, philosophy as he taught it had a 'sort of great freedom, of goodness of mind and even of heart'. Unfortunately there remains nothing of his courses on Hume and Schopenhauer. The essence of the very important course on Descartes is known to us thanks to Étienne Gilson who was his pupil.[1] On the other hand, from his teaching at the Sorbonne Lévy-Bruhl derived two books, one on the philosophy of Jacobi and the other on that of Auguste Comte. A year before this second work moreover, he had published some letters exchanged by the founder of positivism and John Stuart Mill. A few years earlier (in 1880) he had edited Cicero's *De Legibus* and the Nichomachaean Ethics. Then a review, in English, of modern philosophy in France was published by Lévy-Bruhl in the United States. The courses taught at l'École des Sciences politiques were the origin of a volume devoted to *L'Allemagne depuis Leibniz.* But parallel with his teaching which was directed towards the history of ideas, Lévy-

[1] E. Gilson, 'Le Descartes de L. Lévy-Bruhl,' *Revue philosophique*, October–December 1957, pp. 432–451.

Bruhl, a friend of Durkheim, undertook some more personal research in the field of morals and of sociology. Even before the First World War two works appeared which were the outcome of this research and which aroused much interest; these were *La Morale et la science des moeurs* (*Ethics and Moral Science*), and *Les Fonctions mentales dans les sociétés inférieures* (*How Natives Think*).

During the same period, Lévy-Bruhl gave lectures and wrote articles on a very wide range of topics. He contributed to the *Revue bleue*, to the *Revue des deux mondes*, and to the *Revue de Paris*, where in particular he published a study of the philosophy of Gustave Flaubert. In 1881, he sent to the *Nouvelle revue* a text entitled *Henri Heine et la politique contemporaine*. He gave a lecture at Amiens on Turgenev at about the same time, and later he spoke on socialism before the Société industrielle of Mulhouse. In the *Annales de l'École libre des Sciences politiques*, Lévy-Bruhl published many articles, such as: 'Les théories politiques de Frédéric II' (1889) and 'L'influence de Jean-Jacques Rousseau en Allemagne' (July 1887). In 1912, he wrote for the *Revue de métaphysique et de morale* (which devoted a special issue to this author) 'Quelques mots sur la querelle de Hume et de Rousseau'. He also participated very actively in the Universités populaires, and the Minister of Education called on his advice in consultative councils and committees. Further, without being directly affiliated to a party, he took a keen interest in politics. Deeply concerned by the Dreyfus affair, after the first hearing he bore witness in favour of the unjustly accused captain. Moreover the latter was married to a relation of the sociologist. Later, in 1931, Lévy-Bruhl was to recall 'the affair' in the preface to a work entitled *Les Carnets de Schwartzkoppen*. Very close to Jean Jaurès and Lucien Herr, he did not hide his sympathy for socialism, but all those who knew him agree in acknowledging that he was no sectarian and that he never judged people by their opinions. Through friendship for Péguy, as Étienne Gilson reports, he subscribed to *Cahiers de la quinzaine*,[2]

[2] Étienne Gilson, *Le Philosophe et la théologie* (A. Fayard 1960), p. 35.

and later he defended the works of Catholic missions in America, stating that he had been able to ascertain their usefulness in the course of one of his journeys undertaken in the New World under the auspices of the Alliance française.

The qualities of his heart rivalled that of his mind, and Georges Davy, who was his pupil, has summarized in the following words the most marked characteristics of his personality: 'Everything about this master was at one and the same time great and simple. The supreme quality of his person and of his mind was his power of understanding, which was only equalled by his ability to make things comprehensible, and this truly made him a master mind at the same time as a devotee of all the arts.'[3]

He customarily received his friends and pupils on Sunday mornings in his apartment in rue Montalivet and then rue Lincoln. He welcomed everybody without any ostentation, and his conversation had great charm. 'On first meeting', says Albert Rivaud, who succeeded him at the Institute, 'he showed great courtesy. However, he began by presenting to his interlocutor a wall of silence which paralysed the mind. But this, which some might have taken for disdain or boredom, was without doubt only shyness. When he started to speak, he had a sort of hesitation in his voice, a slight dry cough which disappeared little by little. Then he used to warm up if the subject of the conversation was close to his heart. . . . When one knew him better, one enjoyed his quiet irony, a certain British sense of humour.' [4] He had great modesty and when he published in the *Neue freie Zeitung* of Vienna an article devoted to contemporary French philosophy he made no mention of his own works despite their current world renown. The undoubted authority which he had in the university and other places came to him naturally and without effort.

When the First World War broke out, Lévy-Bruhl was too old

[3] G. Davy, *Sociologues d'hier et d'aujourd'hui* (Presses Universitaires de France, 1960, 2nd edition), p. 238.

[4] A. Rivaud, *Notice sur la vie et les travaux de Lucien Lévy-Bruhl* (Institut de France, Académie des Sciences morales et politiques, 1950), pp. 6-7.

for military service, but his intelligence and patriotism found effective employment. The Minister for Munitions, Albert Thomas, who had been his pupil and knew his worth, took him on as an attaché in his cabinet. The great sociologist carried out these duties, which moreover were unpaid, from January 1915 until January 1919. Then, from this date until June 1919, he was attached to the Ministry of Foreign Affairs, where he worked in the Service de Documentation for the Congress of Versailles.

During the war he had contributed actively to the *Bulletin des usines de guerre* and to the *Bulletin de l'Alliance française*, and in 1917 he took over the administration of the *Revue philosophique* which had been founded by Théodule Ribot. That same year he entered the Institut de France as member for the Académie des Sciences morales et politiques. In February 1923 he presented to the Société française de Philosophie a paper, followed by an important discussion, notably with Mauss and Belot, on primitive mentality. In 1925, he created the Institut d'Ethnologie, naming as secretary-generals Paul Rivet and Marcel Mauss, to help him run this organization. In 1927, wishing to devote himself more fully to his researches on primitive mentality, he went into retirement, resigning his chair in the history of modern philosophy at the Sorbonne which, had he wanted, he could certainly have occupied for much longer. In June 1929, he disclosed to the Société française de Philosophie his ideas on the primitive mind, and many philosophers and ethnologists, such as Franz Boas, took part in the discussion.

From 1919 onwards Lucien Lévy-Bruhl's life had been far less sedentary than in previous years. His reputation had spread well beyond the frontiers of France and he received many invitations from foreign universities. Through the Alliance française he did much to spread French culture, for which he was a brilliant ambassador. Missions and lecture tours gave him the chance to visit the distant countries of which he had written in his books, and if he had not the time to do ethnographic work in the course of these journeys, at least he was able to make direct contact with peoples different from those who had moulded his mind.

In 1919–20 he was sent to the United States as an exchange professor at Harvard, and he took advantage of his return journey to tour for the Alliance française, passing through China, Japan, the Philippines, Java, and Indochina. In 1922 he first gave a lecture at Brussels on Descartes and the Cartesian principle, and then devoted the summer to attending the Congress of Americanists which was held in Brazil and where he paid a visit on General Rondon. Afterwards he returned home by way of Paraguay, Bolivia, Argentina (where he gave many lectures), Peru and Chile. In 1923 he went back to Brussels to talk on Pierre Bayle, who was one of his favourite authors, and about Renan. In 1925 he gave a lecture at the university of London, and in 1926 one at The Hague on primitive mentality. Invited in June 1926 to go to the United States for the 50th anniversary of Johns Hopkins University, he delivered the main address on scientific inquiry indicating the importance of basic research in this field. Then in San Francisco, at Berkeley, he gave six lectures on primitive mentality. In March 1928, the opening of university courses at Davos gave him the opportunity to meet Einstein. In the same year he spoke at Berlin and Hamburg, and then once again there was a long tour on behalf of the Alliance française and the Institut d'Ethnologie. From August to October he travelled through many of the Central American countries—Costa Rica, Nicaragua, San Salvador, and Guatemala—in many places attending the founding of ethnological institutes, at Puerto Rico giving a lecture on Graeco=Roman civilization, and at San Salvador a brief sketch of French sociology. In 1930 he spoke in Tunis and then attended the meeting of the International Institute of African Studies before crossing the Atlantic for the fifth time to talk about French philosophy before the Academy of Arts and Letters of New York. The following year he gave, as one of the Herbert Spencer lectures at Oxford, a paper on primitive mentality,[5] then another on the same subject in Copenhagen, and yet others in the Baltic countries. In October 1932 he presided at examinations in Palestine, Egypt, and Syria. In 1934 he

[5] Published by the Clarendon Press, Oxford, in 1931.

devoted a lecture at The Hague to refuting certain criticisms which his theory of primitive mentality had provoked. In 1935 there was a tour of central Europe—to Prague, Vienna and Zurich—with, of course, as his topics primitive mentality and also Comte. In Austria he made the acquaintance of Sigmund Freud. Some months later Lévy-Bruhl returned to Switzerland to speak in Geneva at the International Institute, and then he went to Brussels, to the Congress of the History of Religion.

This superabundant activity did not slow the research and output of our author. As well as his important books devoted to primitive peoples, he wrote articles for various French and foreign periodicals. Among these last we may mention two pieces published in the review *Scientia* edited by Rignano: 'Les causes économiques et politiques de la conflagration européenne' (a work which was afterwards published in the form of a pamphlet in 1915), and 'Les aspects nouveaux de la guerre' (1917), as well as a study entitled 'Primitive mentality and gambling' which appeared in the review *Criterion* in February 1924. Numerous French publications bore witness also to the intensity of his political interests. Already during the war, under the pseudonym Deuzelles (formed from the phonetic transcription of his initials), Lévy-Bruhl had contributed to the journal *L'Humanité* founded by his friend Jaurès, whose memory he honoured in 1916 by publishing some original letters and an intellectual biography under the title 'Quelques pages sur Jaurès'. In the *Revue de Paris*, he tackled some topics on world politics, notably in an article entitled 'L'ébranlement du monde jaune', dated 15th October, 1920. A little before the *Front populaire* came to power in France, he published, in the *Éditions du Progrès civique*, a propaganda pamphlet entitled *L'Idéal républicain*. Moreover, Lévy-Bruhl often met left-wing personalities in the course of receptions at the home of Mme Ménard-Dorian.

During the last years of his life Lévy-Bruhl, always sensitive to the opinions of others, had been led by the criticisms of sociologists and ethnologists to reconsider the very foundations of his conceptions of archaic mentality. In the course of his walks in the avenues of the Bois de Boulogne, at Bagatelle, or else on holiday at the seaside, he jotted in slim notebooks which he kept in his pocket ideas on this subject which came to his mind. His friend, the pastor Maurice Leenhardt, after the death of Lévy-Bruhl, was to publish the contents of these *Carnets*, which make a moving document of the last thoughts of the great sociologist.

The end of his life was overshadowed by the clear awareness which he had of the imminent world disaster. He was at that time, says Albert Rivaud, sad and discouraged. However he retained his brilliant intellect unimpaired until his death on 13th March, 1939.

THE PRINCIPAL WORKS OF LUCIEN LÉVY-BRUHL

L'Idée de responsabilité (Hachette, 1885).

L'Allemagne depuis Leibniz, an essay on the development of German nationalism (Hachette, 1889).

La Philosophie de Jacobi (Alcan, 1894).

History of modern philosophy in France (Chicago, Kegan Paul 1899).

Lettres inédites de John Stuart Mill à Auguste Comte, published together with Comte's replies. Introduction by L. Lévy-Bruhl (Alcan, 1899).

La Philosophie d'Auguste Comte (Alcan, 1900). Translated into German in 1902 and into English in 1903. The 3rd edition revised and corrected in 1913.

La Morale et la science des moeurs (Alcan, 1903). Translated into English in 1905 as *Ethics and Moral Science*. 3rd edition preceded by a new preface, and the 4th edition revised in 1910.

Les Fonctions mentales dans les sociétés inférieures (Alcan, 1910). Translated into English in 1926 as *How Natives Think*.

La Conflagration européenne. Les causes économiques et politiques (Alcan, 1915).

Jean Jaurès (Rieder, 1916). A biographical sketch followed by some unpublished letters.

La Mentalité primitive (Alcan, 1922). Translated into English in 1923 as *Primitive Mentality*.

L'Idéal républicain (*Revue de Paris*, Vol. 1, pp. 805–22, 1924). Reproduced in the form of a pamphlet in the *Éditions du progrès civique*.

L'Âme primitive (Alcan, 1927). Translated into English in 1928 as *The 'Soul' of the Primitive.*

Les Carnets de Schwartzkoppen, the truth about Dreyfus. Edited by Bernhard Schwertfeger and translated from the German by A. Koyré with a preface by Lucien Lévy-Bruhl (Presses Universitaires de France, 1930).

Le Surnaturel et la nature dans la mentalité primitive (Alcan, 1931). Translated into English in 1935 as *Primitives and the Supernatural.*

La Mythologie primitive (Alcan, 1935).

L'Expérience mystique et les symboles chez les primitifs (Alcan, 1938).

Les Carnets de Lévy-Bruhl (Presses Universitaires de France, 1949). Posthumous work with a preface by Maurice Leenhardt. English translation by Peter Rivière in preparation, Oxford, Blackwell.

Lévy-Bruhl. Morceaux choisis (Gallimard, 1936).

THE PHILOSOPHY OF LUCIEN LÉVY-BRUHL

I. FROM PHILOSOPHY TO SOCIOLOGY

The works which Lucien Lévy-Bruhl devoted to the history of philosophy, particularly those on German thought, on Comte, and on Jacobi, deserve to be analysed because he shows in the discussion of others the stamp of his own original mind. But posterity will remember him even more by the books in which he reveals his own doctrine directly. From this point of view, *La Morale et la science des moeurs* is a very important work and may mark the turning point in the development which led Lévy-Bruhl from pure philosophy to the sociology of primitive peoples.

There are two aspects—one negative, the other positive—to this book. First, Lévy-Bruhl endeavours to demonstrate the impossibility and uselessness of all moral theory which he calls metamorals. Moreover this criticism applies as much to allegedly scientific ethics (biological, psychological, or sociological) as to metaphysical ethics, because both equally purport to be at the same time theoretical and normative, to give knowledge and prescription, and these things are incompatible. Theory can concern itself with what is, not with what ought to be. The proof of the uselessness of metamorals is largely provided by the fact that all moral theories, despite their different bases, agree in their practical precepts. For example, the utilitarianism of Stuart Mill has a strong tendency to result in the same moral rules as the Gospel. Hence, metamorals can only build theories on existing customs without being able to influence them. Finally, moral theory rests on two false assumptions. On the one hand, it supposes in effect that human nature is always and everywhere the same, whereas it varies according to civilizations. On the other hand, it reasons as if moral conscience were a harmonious whole, when in fact it harbours contradictions, amalgamating precepts deriving from different sources.

Having discredited moral theories, Lévy-Bruhl lays the foundations for the positive science of morals which ought to replace them. This science, like physics, ought to stick to purely objective facts, and to look for their laws instead of trying to interpret them. The science of morals, of which philologists and linguists, followed by economists, experimental psychologists and historians were the forerunners, does not claim to 'found' morality, but restricts itself to the analysis of the moral reality which, though familiar, is often unknown. At one and the same time it ought to take account of sentiments and attitudes which are facts. On this science of morals could be founded a rational discipline which, as with every technique, would assume an existing knowledge. The laws thus established will be valid only in a given sociological context; in particular they will have the advantage of eliminating anachronistic duties.

Thus the basic principle of this book was that human morality ought to be made the object of a truly scientific study, and that to this end it is necessary to recognize its relativity. Having criticized the postulate that human nature is invariable, Lévy-Bruhl allocated as sociology's prime task the objective examination of the variations of human nature according to type of civilization.

Moreover he was a rationalist and perhaps he also wanted—the better to isolate rational thought in all its purity—to see how everything in mankind's intellectual behaviour which seemed to deviate from this ideal could be explained sociologically.

Finally, as he himself related, he became interested more directly in the problem of modes of thought when in 1903 his friend from the École normale supérieure, Chavannes, sent him a translation of ancient Chinese philosophers. He read it and was amazed to find the text incomprehensible. He then came to wonder if there were not modes of thought which were impenetrable to each other.

He started to read some ethnographic works, and he noted a strong affinity between the ways of thought of all primitive peoples. At the same time, he found a great difference between this mentality and our own. He therefore thought that before undertaking the inventory of all mental diversities, sociology had some chance of making the problem clearer by first applying itself to a comparison of the two sorts of mentality which obviously must be the most different: that of primitive peoples and that of peoples fashioned by a rationalist culture. And it is to this end that he devoted the six volumes which made him the sociologist of primitive mentality. But he was not a man to allow himself to be imprisoned by his own theory, and, as he advanced in this study, he was led to clarify or to modify his concepts in order to take better account of the evidence which he collected. In particular there seems to be an especially clear progression between the first three and the last three works in this series.

II. THE THEORY OF PRIMITIVE MENTALITY

Les Fonctions mentales, *La Mentalité primitive* and *L'Âme primitive*, expound his doctrine in its most pronounced form.

(A) *The problem and the method.* What is the nature of the differences between modes of thought? Lévy-Bruhl here opposes the so-called animist school (of Frazer and Tylor) for whom the functions of the mind are the same everywhere, but are simply used in the wrong way by primitive peoples, in such a way that our mind, with its categories, would lead to the same result if we were in the place of 'savages' with a science as backward as theirs. On the contrary, according to Lévy-Bruhl, the difference is fundamental, not fortuitous: primitive peoples do not reason badly, but they think differently from us. It is necessary, in order to understand them, to rid ourselves of our mental processes. Of course, there are some features common to all species of thought, but mental operations cannot be reduced to a single type. How does it come about then that primitive peoples think differently from us, since it is not by the failure of individual reasoning? The answer is clear: it is because the social group fashions minds in a different way. For Lévy-Bruhl the problem is collective, and thus sociological. Thus one could, he thinks, construct a collective psychology for each society. The first stage in this work consists, as we have seen, in studying the societies furthest away from our forms of thought, that is to say those which are characterized by the lack of abstraction or conceptualization. They correspond, broadly, to societies without writing. How can we get to know these 'primitive' peoples? Through the works of ethnographers and even through the writings of travellers and missionaries. Some authors, such as Evans-Pritchard, object to this evidence as being misleading, because the writers in question have noted what struck them, whatever seemed to them unusual, leaving out the commonplace aspects of primitive peoples' lives and thus exaggerating the difference between them and us. To this, Lévy-Bruhl replies that this does not present a drawback because his aim is not to provide us with a complete picture of archaic existence, but to highlight the differences between the primitive mentality and ours. If Lévy-Bruhl schematizes and even seems at times to caricature the thought of preliterate peoples, he does it intentionally and knowingly.

(B). *The characteristics of primitive mentality.* The problem of modes of thought, as Lévy-Bruhl poses it, leads first to the examination of *collective representations.* By that is meant discerning the ways of grasping reality common to the members of a given social group. Although such collective representations do not exist apart from individuals, they are imposed on the latter and cannot be explained by purely individual psychology. Moreover the word 'representation' as Lévy-Bruhl intends it (influenced by Ribot's psychology of emotions) does not indicate a purely intellectual phenomenon because, particularly in the case of primitive peoples, representations are intermingled with affective elements.

The characteristic of the collective representations of primitive peoples which clearly differentiates them from concepts is that they are *mystical*. This means, not that they involve a religious mysticism in the modern sense, but that they assume 'the belief in forces, influences and actions imperceptible to the senses but nevertheless real'. The mystical collective representations of primitive peoples are not simply connected with perception by association; they form an integral part of it. It is in this that they differ from our present superstitions. For example, primitive man directly perceives an animal together with its magical powers and its mythical meanings. In his world there is no line of demarcation between the natural and the supernatural.

The difference between the mentality of primitive people and our own derives not only from the mystical character of their collective representations, but also from the way in which these representations are interconnected. This does not mean that they obey a logic other than our own, because the two mentalities are not totally unintelligible to each other. Lévy-Bruhl is quite precise on this point, as certain of his detractors who have wrongly attributed to him a theory based on two different logics seem to have forgotten. From his first works on primitive mentality, Lévy-Bruhl clearly shows that it is not guided by a logic different from ours, but that he thinks that it does not exclusively obey the laws of our logic. It is in this sense that he calls it *prelogical*. It by no means follows that it is held to be para-logical or anti-logical; nor does it mean that it constitutes in the evolution of thought a stage prior to the appearance of logical thought. 'In calling it prelogical,' writes Lévy-Bruhl, 'I wish only to say that it does not tie itself down, as our thought does, to the avoidance of contradiction before all else.' In fact this mentality obeys a principle which is not radically opposed to that of non-contradiction, but which is simply indifferent to it. It is this principle which Lévy-Bruhl calls the *law of participation*. By virtue of this law, things can be at the same time themselves and something else, and they can be joined by connections having nothing in common with those of our logic. What Tylor and

Frazer explained by animism is in reality an effect of participation. In the perception of primitive man animate or inanimate beings share certain powers. It is only in societies already somewhat evolved that these powers are thought of as souls. In the primitive universe, there is rather a *continuum* of powers (*mana*).

It would be a mistake to try to make two clear divisions in the thought of primitive man: the logical individual representation on the one hand, and the collective mystical and prelogical representation on the other. In reality the mental activity of primitive man is totally socialized and within it the logical and the prelogical coexist. This, as Lévy-Bruhl recognizes, makes the analysis of primitive mentality very difficult. Nevertheless, by starting from the fundamental characteristics which have just been brought out, it is not impossible to undertake its description.

Because logical and prelogical workings are closely intertwined in his mind, primitive man is far less able than we are to abstract and to generalize. Things and beings which participate in one another form totalities which are perceived in a more qualitative than quantitative fashion, and the qualities themselves cannot easily be isolated from the beings to which they are attached. This is shown clearly in numeration among primitive peoples: for them, numbers are rather forms of qualitative distinction, and this brings about some peculiarities in the language of 'savages'. Their vocabulary is very rich and copious because it is so unabstract, and this makes the role of the memory more important. Sign language expressing positions and movements must come to the help of the symbolic system which, in spite of its superabundance, is not enough to specify everything qualitatively.

(C) *The world and man according to primitive mentality.* In his representation of the world, primitive man orients himself differently from us, more particularly because he has not the same conception of causality. The main principle behind this difference is that primitive mentality neglects secondary causes in favour of mystical ones. What for us is a true cause is for primitive man merely an event involving mystical forces. Of course, this occasionalist concept of causality is very far from that of Malebranche, for what primitive man seeks behind appearances is not the metaphysical reason for things but occult powers. However, here it is clear that we would be wrong to accuse primitive people of poor reasoning when they are simply reasoning differently. Even Malebranche sought for the real cause beyond the level of appearances, and belonged to the tradition of Cartesian and Platonic philosophy which finds explanation beyond the perceptible properties. The occasionalism of primitive people is the direct result of the mystical character of their collective representations; the action of supernatural forces is a prime datum in their perception. This is why, for example, they attribute the misfortune of premature death not to natural causes but to sorcery. Likewise, every accident appears as a revelation; nothing is fortuitous. Mystical causality, the most valid from their point of view, is not grasped by inference or reasoning, but is given intuitively through the 'preconnexions' which establish a direct route between this sense perception and that invisible force. As the mystical cause is extra-spatial and extra-temporal, it follows that time and space, in this conception, have nothing to do with the homogeneous quanta by which we represent them, but are, in a sense, closer to Bergson's 'experiential duration'.

This representation of the world, albeit different from our own, does not prevent preliterate people from achieving, sometimes very well, technical activities which make use of genuine causality. But, says Lévy-Bruhl, this does not at all imply a clear knowledge of such causality. The man who constructs a canoe in order to put it in the water does not need to have learned Archimedes' principle which he nevertheless puts to use. He acts by intuition, just like a billiards player who, without knowing geometry, without having to think, plays the stroke which is necessary for a given position of the balls. Thus primitive people, even if they are capable of actions comparable with ours, have a picture of the world which is very different from that which our science gives us.

It is the same with the 'prenotions' which they have of their souls and their own persons. Like a child—but in a way which does not allow the comparison to be pushed too far—primitive man has a sense of his personal existence, but does not possess a clear idea of Self. He does not see himself as a creature distinct from the beings and things which surround him. He does not think of the universe as formed from separate substances; for him all beings are the receptacles of that anonymous and impersonal form which the anthropologists call *mana*. There is, therefore, an essential homogeneity, a kinship of essence between all things, animate or inanimate. The spiritual is not distinct from the material.

Furthermore, primitive mentality does not separate the individual from the species to which it belongs, and, as far as man is concerned, does not conceive of the individual separate from the group. This appears clearly in totemism. In short the body is not distinguished from the mind, and the self is not confined within the boundaries of the body but extends to what Lévy-Bruhl calls the *appurtenances* (for example, hair, footprints, and clothing). The relationship of participation between the individual and his appurtenances is not the result of a transfer of ideas or feelings, like that which we make between a man and his photograph, but is directly felt by primitive man. It is according to this principle of appurtenance that we must interpret the primitive notions which we translate by the words soul, double, shadow, reflection, etc. In this mentality there is a distinction between one and two and even between one and several—duality is not incompatible with the fundamental unity of the individual. In this way are explained the beliefs involving the ubiquity or the splitting of the individual in a dream. The analysis of beliefs and rituals concerned with death shows all this; the whole group is affected by the death of one of its members; the deceased is supposed to enter the world of the dead while still remaining united to the corpse. This is further proved by the function of names. A name gives the individual his personality by joining him to the group; it is attached to him as an appurtenance; often a newborn child is given the name of an ancestor who, it is believed, lives again in him.

To sum up, in primitive mentality mystical and prelogical collective representations and the principle of participation make the whole conception of Self and of the world different from ours. If primitive people stagnate in this manner of thinking, it is because the mystical nature of their mentality makes it *impervious to experience*, that is to say insensitive to the contradictions which objectively observed facts would seem to present to their beliefs. It is also because they are collectively opposed to all innovation. Misoneism is an essential feature of their way of being. However, if this partly explains why certain peoples have remained tied to the primitive mentality, the relationship between that and the civilized mentality poses some delicate problems.

(D) *Primitive mentality and civilized mentality.* Lévy-Bruhl looked for intermediaries between these two terms, and although he rejected the idea of a rectilinear evolution proceeding from the prelogical to the logical, he envisaged, at the very heart of the primitive world, a succession of stages which make the transition from one type of civilization to another more conceivable. Indeed, among preliterate societites, those which are sometimes called simpler, there are those in which participation is already no longer directly felt and experienced, but becomes an intermediary representation. From this stage onwards the individual no longer says, for example, that he *is* an animal, but that such a totemic animal is his ancestor. Myths and symbols then become essential, for without them participations could no longer be conceived. One is thus already on the road that leads to the concept, particularly when the cognitive element is detached from affective factors. The preconnexions which from the beginning made perception mystical, lose their force, and one becomes sensitive to contradictions and the teachings of experience. Certainly there is not always a continuous evolution between the truly primitive stage (that of the Australians, for example) dominated by perceived participation and the already more evolved state (that of the American Indians, for example) in which the sacred is distinguished from the profane. However the important thing is that, at the end of these transformations, sometimes interrupted by checks and regressions, can be found a transition from truly primitive mentality to conceptual thought.

One might then wonder whether, in diverging from primitiveness, societies do not manage, at the other extreme, to free themselves of it totally. In fact, says Lévy-Bruhl, the mystical mentality never completely disappears. Concepts can only be developed from collective representations, and these always leave a certain residue of mystical elements. Moreover, the concept cannot in all cases be separated from an affective and emotional aura. Finally, since the mystical mentality is not hostile but simply indifferent to logical thought, it is possible for the former to exist and to maintain a feeling of experiential participation, even if the latter progresses indefinitely. Coexistence is thus possible. Lévy-Bruhl adds that mystical thought responds to a need in human nature, for rational knowledge cannot be fully satisfying. It separates the subject from its object too much. For example, the notion of God which it can construct does not replace the feeling of participation in the divine.

In short, there is indeed a social evolution which proceeds from a maximum of primitive mentality to a maximum of conceptual and rational thought. But, just as among the most primitive peoples the logic of non-contradiction has its place at the centre of a mentality which is sometimes indifferent to it, so, inversely, the advance of civilization will never be able to make the mystical mentality disappear completely. Lévy-Bruhl's doctrine is not that of a prelogic representing a non-rational stage; he does not subscribe to a doctrine of two mutually exclusive mentalities. Nevertheless, the analysis of collective representations among primitive peoples allowed him to analyse a mode of thought which exists among us but which, among us, would be more difficult to observe.

After the three books containing the themes just summarized Lévy-Bruhl continued his study of primitive mentality, but felt the need to use some new concepts and to clarify his position on certain points. This was because his theory had been much criticized, and his open, undogmatic mind made it possible for him to profit from objections. In 1926 and 1927, several writers, such as Larguier des Bancels, Raoul Allier and Édouard Leroy, had reproached Lévy-Bruhl for having exaggerated the differences between primitive people and ourselves. As early as 1912, Durkheim, in *Formes élémentaires de la vie religieuse* (p. 269) disputed the possibility of a thought which was not conceptual and complained that Lévy-Bruhl had confused the concept with generalization, because, as he said, to conceive is not to generalize but to subsume the variable under the constant, the individual under the social. Further, Mauss who, at the Société française de Philosophie, criticized the application of the wide term primitive to some very diverse peoples, endeavoured in his *Essai sur le don* (1924), to centre his study on total social phenomena and criticized as being too strongly contrasted distinctions between different sectors, such as technology, science and religion. In 1922, the theses of Georges Davy in *La foi jurée* clearly showed that one could be aware of the role of participation among primitive people while still remaining faithful to the Durkheimian view which seeks to explain the present and rational forms of thought by more rudimentary collective phenomena. Lastly, in 1927, Essertier claimed to find the principle of primitive mentality in a need to explain, a need held in common with the scientific mind but which the primitive mentality tried to satisfy by inventing causes.

In short, the first three works which Lévy-Bruhl had devoted to primitive people had awakened considerable interest everywhere, and had aroused various thoughts, objections and interpretations. Sometimes the author had certainly been misunderstood, and then he had to explain himself in greater detail; sometimes he had provoked questions for which he had to find answers.

III. PRIMITIVE MENTALITY AND AFFECTIVITY

In the last three books which he devoted to primitive mentality (*Le Surnaturel et la nature; La Mythologie primitive;*

L'Expérience mystique et les symboles chez les primitifs) Lévy-Bruhl refined and qualified his thought. At the same time, sensitive perhaps to the critcisms of Mauss, he outlined a change of method. Instead of borrowing his examples at random from very disparate sources covering all preliterate peoples, as he had done in the preceding works, he tried first of all to centre attention on a chosen ethnographic area, either in a radical way (as in *La Mythologie primitive*, which is concerned solely with the Australians and Papuans), or in a more flexible way, making some comparisons with other regions (as in *Le Surnaturel et la nature*). But in his last book (*L'Expérience mystique* . . .) he preferred to return to a comparison extended to cover all the 'primitive' peoples of the world, though proving more circumspect in the choice of sources than he had been at the start.

In this second phase, his doctrine is not exactly transformed but he shows it in a slightly different light. In effect, although Lévy-Bruhl does not completely abandon any of his key concepts (mysticism, prelogical thought, participation, and occasionalism) the order of their importance is no longer quite the same, because now the mystical character prevails over prelogic. Moreover, a new idea appears which tends to dominate and explain the others.

(A) *The principles of primitive mentality*. Some refinements are made concerning the indifference of primitive mentality to contradition, an indifference which does not preclude a possible realization of the latter. For example, the Eskimos relate that the 'mother of the Caribou', the mythical creator of this species of animal, wore trousers of caribou hide. When his attention is drawn to this point, the Eskimo recognizes that there is a contradiction in this myth! How could this clothing have existed before the caribou had come into the world? But this logical difficulty, though recognized, does not impede belief. Without doubt, says Lévy-Bruhl, 'the fundamental structure of the human mind is the same everywhere'; but the prelogical attitude allows the admission of contradictions. This is accounted for by the mystical orientation of those minds which attach but little importance to the physical or logical conditions of the possibility of things, and also by the fact that primitive thought conceptualizes so little. Certainly the 'savage' has concepts, but they are less systematized than ours. The knowledge of primitive people is not classified rationally—it is 'unpackaged'. Since items of knowledge remain thus simply juxtaposed, the field stays open to mystical preconnexions, and contradictions have little hope of being disclosed or rejected. Finally it is the emotional element which compensates for logical generality.

In the last three works of Lévy-Bruhl one also sees the postulate of impermeability to experience being supplanted by that of a fusion between mystical experience and ordinary experience. Certainly primitive man can broadly distinguish between the natural and the supernatural worlds. But often his experience jumps abruptly from one to the other. The supernatural indeed belongs to 'another world', but one which is not isolated from the natural world and which can, on the contrary, intervene at any moment. This is quite in agreement with the occasionalism of primitive thought, and basically everything happens as if primitive man mixes up the two worlds even if he is capable of distinguishing them. It is for this reason that nothing is absurd to him since nothing is incompatible with the data of an experience in which the visible realities and the intervention of supernatural powers are intertwined. In these conditions, the prelogical character of primitive mentality becomes secondary when compared with its mystical nature.

The mystical experience which, in the last analysis, explains this mentality deserves the name of experience on condition that this term is not given the purely cognitive meaning to which philosophers, from Plato to the post-Kantians, have accustomed us. If the experience of primitive people is mystical, it is just because it is not purely intellectual but principally affective, and because its essential function is not to inform the subject about the real properties of things and beings. So if the prelogical is explained by the mystical, it must now be added that the mystical results from the predominance of affectivity in experience.

Emotion and sentiment give primitive man a knowledge of reality other than that given to him by purely objective experience. Thus the category of the supernatural is of the affective order, and Lévy-Bruhl now introduces a new notion into his analysis—that of the *affective category of the supernatural*—to designate the element common to all mystical representations, what it is they all share. This is more felt than known and is not to be found at the level of ideas. In this Lévy-Bruhl brings an important modification into philosophy which, since Aristotle, has limited categories of thought to the intellect, disregarding whatever comes from affectivity. This new category presents itself as a particular colouring or tone of certain representations. It is because it is at once general and emotive that it can be called the 'affective category'. Primitive man does not need an intellectual act in order to recognize this special tonality when the affective category of the supernatural comes into play.

It might be thought that its diffuse nature is difficult to grasp owing to the diversity of supernatural beings. This objection would have some value if one considered the Greek and Latin mythologies, for example, in which the deities are clearly individualized. But, among primitive peoples, representations of the supernatural are very vague. The occasionalism of this mentality tends simply to make invisible powers the essential principle of whatever happens. They are revealed by their continual influence, but they themselves remain blurred and very varied—as great gods, spirits of trees, of animals, of the dead, sorcerers, demons, etc. All these create a fairly indistinct totality towards which the characteristic emotional tone is fear.

It is the unusual which reveals the intervention of these agents, and thereby involves the affective category of the supernatural, because primitive man only feels himself protected from fear in an unchanging order. Everything which is abnormal, unusual, strange, new, accidental, or bizarre, troubles him and seems to forbode ill. Although one could find fear of the unusual even among animals, in the mystical experience of primitive men there is more than this quasi-instinctive reaction, and social elements play an essential role. The unusual is thus the direct manifestation, in experience, of the affective category of the supernatural mobilized both by a natural and psychological emotion and by collective representations.

(B) *Representations and beliefs*, How is the supernatural represented? What are the principle beliefs related to it? To answer these questions, one must first look at the vaguest aspects of the supernatural, then at its means of revelation, before coming to myths and symbols.

Among primitive peoples, it is the emotions which enter most directly into the affective category, that of fear in particular, which results in the search for a defence. Therefore, what matters first about supernatural forces is what they indicate and, consequently, their good or bad dispositions. Primitive man feels menaced by a crowd of malign influences, which is why he needs a large number of remedies and amulets which are themselves vehicles of mystical, although benevolent, forces. The unusual can also be lucky sometimes. Likewise there are people who bring fortune or misfortune.

Because objects and beings in the primitive world are the loci of good or bad dispositions, one might be tempted to resort to the animist explanation. But once again Lévy-Bruhl denounces the errors of this theory which makes primitive man a civilized one reasoning badly and which judges his habits of thought according to ours. In reality, the good or bad dispositions of beings and of things are not inevitably conceived of as psychic and do not presuppose the notion of soul. Likewise, propitiatory rites towards animals, the totemic ceremonies of the *intichiuma* type whose aim is to influence animals or plants or even natural phenomena, do not always summon a sort of soul or spirit from these things and beings.

How do the supernatural powers reveal themselves? Spontaneously through the unusual, as we have said, but there are also more elaborate means and more special cases. Notably these are luck and magic, dreams and visions, and the presence of the dead.

When something unusual or unexpected happens, what concerns primitive men is to know if what we call luck is for or against them. Revelations of this type, by interrupting the normal order of nature, mobilize the mystical experience. This explains why, as we have already seen, a misfortune is never perceived as fortuitous; for example, if lightning strikes a hut one looks for the sorcerer who has provoked it by his actions. Or else, in other cases, such an accident will be attributed to the violation of a taboo which has irritated the supernatural powers. To avert misfortune these powers can be addressed directly, but more often there is recourse to magic which, in practice, is mixed up with practical and technical procedures. For example, in the art of the healer there can be found at one and the same time rudiments of medicine (recourse to empirical remedies) and magical actions. Likewise, when constructing a canoe, a man is not satisfied with making it, sometimes very skilfully, according to a technique which allows it to float well, but must add incantations to avert bad luck, especially if it is to be used on the open sea. Magic arises when there is a risk, when technique does not in itself offer a sufficient guarantee. Thus, in competitive sports, magic plays a great part because there are hazards, despite the fact of physical superiority. In games of chance, this is still more evident since here the part played by skill may be reduced to nothing. The action of invisible powers then appears decisive to the extent that the game of chance itself constitutes a privileged mystical experience. It is a means of putting to the test the amulets, incantations and rites on which one ordinarily counts for protection against bad luck. In this sense, one can compare the game with an act of divination, or again with those ordeals whose importance Lévy-Bruhl repeatedly emphasized. Moreover many divinatory procedures resemble games of chance or competition.

Dreams and visions are another characteristic domain of the mystical experience where the affective category of the supernatural can be clearly seen to enter. Primitive men are capable of establishing a distinction between dream and waking life, but they do not place the former outside reality as we normally do.

For them, dreams are revelations, just like omens. In many cases they let themselves be guided by the indications which they believe they find in their dream fantasies. Dream, among these peoples, is allied to myth, and such is the prestige of the dream and such its power of mystical suggestion that, even today, it retains for certain people its value as a privileged experience.

Finally, another important mode of revelation of supernatural forces is the presence of the dead already perceived in certain dreams, but which can also, among primitive peoples, make itself felt in a state of wakefulness. Although rare this experience is considered as possible and as real as others. The deceased may reveal himself in different ways, either in the form of an animal, or as a ghost, or in relation to a material object, a skull for example.

We have just seen in what ways occult powers become objects of experience, but what is their nature? It is here that myths and symbols come in.

Lévy-Bruhl sharply criticizes the aetiological interpretation of myths which, like the animist theory, attributes to primitive men a reasoning of the same type as ours. In reality, he says, for primitive man the supernatural world is not the result of intellectual effort but the object of direct experience.

In studying the beliefs of Australians and Papuans, Lévy-Bruhl shows that the mythology of primitive peoples is not organized, but that, despite the incoherent and scattered character of the myths, they have in common an inspiration and a homogeneity of tone which must be attributed to a certain uniformity of emotion, that is to say to the general character of the affective category of the supernatural.

Myth is situated in a special time; it is 'meta-historical' and above all creative, so that it is future as well as past. It is in this sense that mythical ancestors are distinguished from real ancestors, and it is the former who created what exists today. They belong outside time.

The mythical world is characterized by fluidity of images and by metamorphoses. Everything is possible in that world; categories there are not separate, so that beings can be at one and the same time human and animal. For primitive man this constitutes reality *par excellence*, at one and the same time prenatural and supernatural. This world makes its influence felt in actual experience, and moreover there are beings, men (sorcerers and shamans) or animals which, more than others, have the power to participate in this superior reality.

It can happen, certainly, that myths help to explain what is, but such is not their primary function. They reflect the supernatural and they have a value which is at one and the same time transcendental and live-giving. It is by reference to this role of myth that totemism, with its beliefs and its rites, can be understood. For example, the totemic relationship derives from the myth which creates an identity of essence between a social group and an animal species that have been produced, in the period of meta-history, by a common ancestor.

Knowledge of myths itself creates a participation, and in certain cases it is confined to initiates because it confers power. The recitation of myths, their graphic representation, and their ritual dramatization are means of activating the force which this participation furnishes. Moreover it is thus that the representations, half-anthromorphic and half-animal, which are found in prehistoric caves can be explained. Palaeolithic men had myths which provided them with magical models.

The myth, presenting itself as a model, creates a precedent. It is in this sense that certain myths serve to explain misfortunes, such as, for example, attributing the origin of death to the disobedience of an ancestor. However, it must be understood, as Lévy-Bruhl insists, that myth does not explain in order to satisfy intellectual curiosity, but simply to demonstrate the intervention of the supernatural in the course of experience. Accordingly it turns aside from empirical causal explanations, and serves rather to justify, to legitimate, by relating present events to archetypes and by effecting a sort of projection into the past. The allegedly mythical explanation is a direct contact with the invisible powers, and it is also a means of participating in these powers by the rites which evoke them, by virtue of what Lévy-Bruhl calls 'the scheme of imitation-participation'.

The function of symbols is situated at a different level from that of myths. The reality in which primitive men live is a double one; on the one hand there is that reality in which they note the regular sequences of phenomena, and on the other the invisible reality where the supernatural powers reign. But these do not form two separate domains; they 'come together in a unique and global experience where the positive or ordinary experience... and the mystical experience are present at one and the same time'. However, the supernatural reality, which preoccupies primitive men more than the other, comes to them in another way, not as knowledge, but through experience of an affective character, although emotion here blends into a complex of representative elements determined by the tradition of the social group.

Just as with ordinary experience, primitive man is naturally inclined to portray to himself in a tangible way the present and invisible reality of his mystical experience. But to grasp the intangible, what was pure relevation must become concrete experience by modelling itself on the concrete world, by becoming objective. This is one of the essential functions of symbols; the invisible power is represented by a visible being. But, as unity and duality are not mutually exclusive in primitive mentality, these two beings are but one, and the link of participation which unites them is directly felt. At the very least, this is how it is in very primitive societies where, for example, the appurtenance *is* truly the being with which it participates, and in this case symbolism properly speaking does not yet exist, but a veritable unity-duality. It is only when participation ceases to be felt directly that there is a symbol. Thus, in totemism, as long as the members of the clan directly perceive the identity of essence between man and his totem, the latter could not be considered as the symbol of the clan, as Durkheim seems to believe. It is only when this feeling of identity changes into a feeling of kinship that the totem becomes the emblem of the clan. Thus Durkheim's theory is applicable only to this secondary phase of evolution whose principle Lévy-Bruhl had already indicated in his first works. It is true that, even at this stage, we are still far from conceptualization, for when participation is represented by symbolism instead of being lived directly the symbol is not for all that a simple label; it is still imbued with the participation which expresses itself through the symbol and which confers on it its sacred character.

(C) *Action and rites.* How does primitive man behave with regard to the supernatural? There are simple actions and others which are more elaborate.

The imitation-perception scheme is used in certain forms of magic, either directly or else under the form of symbolic prefiguration. Thus one can act on the symbol of a thing as if one were acting directly on the thing itself, or else use symbol-appurtenances, initiate the transfer of qualities, using formulae and words magically. All this is readily explained by participation.

The more complex rituals come down to the same principle. This participation does not imply belief in individual beings, for the representations can remain vague. The aim of many of the ceremonies is not, as is sometimes believed, to serve material interests, but to create a participation between man and the supernatural powers. In particular, such is the role of masks, which make present the beings embodying these forces. Equally, ecstasy is above all a means of reinforcing participation, which may go as far as 'possession'.

Despite the precautions which primitive man takes to assure the benevolence of invisible powers, it can happen that he is obliged to realize that he has failed. Most often he seeks the reason for this in sorcery, by virtue of his occasionalist conception of causality. And against sorcery he has recourse to certain rites, in particular rites of purification, which can take very different forms. To guard against impurity there are also rites of protection, notably taboos. Other practices are intended to thwart inauspicious manoeuvres or events and even to annul them.

(D) *From pre-religion to folklore.* From all the beliefs and practices of primitive peoples one can abstract certain 'constants' which order the connexions between concrete reality and a mythical world peopled by fluid images of culture-heroes.

Among certain peoples, an evolution from this truly archaic base can be noted: the ancestral culture-heroes tend to assume a fixed personality, to become divinities; men no longer believe that their existence depends strictly on ceremonies which actualize the participation with the mythical world. From then onwards one may speak of a religion, whereas very archaic beliefs and practices represent rather a *pre-religion*. In using this term, Lévy-Bruhl indicates his disagreement with Durkheim, for whom religion is always basically the same, whether among Australian tribes or in western societies. Yet Lévy-Bruhl recognizes that the passage from pre-religion to religion is not made abruptly and without certain survivals (for example, divinities in animal form).

Nevertheless, even when religion is far removed from the constants of pre-religion, the fluidity of the mythical world does not disappear completely from the imagination; it survives in folk tales. These stories, which are no longer the object of true belief, please and charm us because they answer to a natural inclination of our mind: we need relaxation, because the civilized mentality and rational thought exact a real tension.

IV. THE EVENTUAL REFINEMENTS

From the six books which Lévy-Bruhl devoted to primitive mentality there emerges a coherent doctrine, but one open to various interpretations. Because the author has often paid attention to the transition between the truly primitive state of thought and the modern mentality, it is only with difficulty that every evolutionist perspective can be excluded. But, in affirming that primitive mentality, on the one hand, and rational mentality, on the other, are both in varying degrees present in every human mind, Lévy-Bruhl confirms the structuralist interpretations put upon his doctrine by Émile Bréhier and Van der Leeuw. Briefly, what has been described to us under the name of primitive mentality is undoubtedly a permanent structure of the human mind, but in our society this structure is blurred by the supremacy of scientific thought, whereas it remains in the foreground among preliterate peoples. Such, at least, is the position which seems clearly affirmed in the posthumous *Carnets*.

Another uncertainty may still arise about what remains of the prelogical character of primitive mentality after the last explanation has been sought in the affective category. Certainly Lévy-Bruhl had, from the beginning, precisely stated that he did not at all want to suggest the idea of a 'prelogic' prior to the advent of logic. But it is nonetheless true that the first books posed the problem of the differences between the mentalities in terms of logic. At the very least the hypothesis of different mental habits was adduced. In the later works it seems that the discovery of the affective category even modifies the way of asking the question. The description of archaic mentality is no longer so much that of specific characteristics of the mind, constituent or acquired, as that of the role of affectivity in thought. Again this is clearly confirmed in the *Carnets*, where Lévy-Bruhl irrevocably abandons the term 'prelogic'. Henceforth he affirms that 'the logical structure of the human mind is the same everywhere.' This is why, instead of pointing out, as he did earlier, the 'contradictions' to which the primitive mentality is supposed to be indifferent, he prefers to speak only of 'incompatibilities' of which it takes no account. Moreover it should not be said that this mentality does not conceptualize, but only that it grants more importance than does ours to the affective meaning of symbols and concepts.

The most important point is the distinction between the two sorts of experience, one of which is called 'mystical' but which could just as well have been called 'mythical'. It is this which makes primitive men insensitive to certain incompatibilities. If one wishes to search for the ultimate explanation of mystical experience, one will find the affective category of the supernatural, although to be precise the very term 'category' no longer seems very suitable for the author of the *Carnets*, since it is too reminiscent of logic.

In conclusion, from this rich body of work, which was inspired by the anxiety to take ever better account of the facts, there are three main achievements to be remembered: firstly, new light thrown on humanity in general; then the appeal to affectivity to explain all that seems most mysterious in primitive mentality; and finally, a clearly pluralist method of investigation which boldly restated many problems.

EXTRACTS

AGAINST THE POSTULATE OF THE IDENTITY OF HUMAN NATURE

La Morale et la science des moeurs (1903), pp. 75–9

From now on, we can no longer represent the whole of humanity, from the psychological and moral point of view, as so similar to the part which we know from our direct experience that we can dispense with studying the rest. One day, perhaps, sociology will be able to determine precisely what there is in common among the individuals of all human groups. At the moment a more modest task presents itself. First it is necessary to analyse, with the greatest possible rigour, the rich variety which is open to observation and which, today, we have no means of reducing to a unity. Are we not even unable to conceive—let alone realize—a universal history? Since we have rejected the philosophies of history which provide a unifying principle in the form of theological or at least teleological ideas, the conception of humanity as a whole escapes us. In the present state of our knowledge there is only the unity of an aggregate—a plurality of civilizations, each exhibiting its own characteristics and appearing to have undergone an independent development.

The history of anthropology places us in the presence of an infinitely varied and complex reality, and we are indeed forced to recognize that we shall acquire a knowledge of it only at the price of long, methodical and collective efforts, as in the case of the natural phenomena presented to our senses. As soon as we contemplate societies different from that in which everything seems clear to us because everything is familiar, we meet at every step problems which we are incapable of resolving by common sense, aided only by thought and by current knowledge of 'human nature'. The facts which disconcert us surely obey laws, but what are they? We cannot guess. In one sense, social reality presents more difficulties to scientific research than does the physical world, because, even supposing that static laws are known, the state of society at any given moment is never intelligible except through the prior evolution of which it is the present outcome; and how rare are the cases where the historical knowledge of this past is so complete and so certain that nothing indispensable is missing!

Moreover, this is yet another reason for never straying from a scrupulously objective method, and for us to expect that here, as in the science of physical nature, what is likely is often not the truth. D'Alembert amused himself by formulating a certain number of physical laws which, *a priori*, would seem to us not only acceptable but very probably true—if experiment did not demonstrate their falsity. 'The barometer rises to foretell rain.' As a matter of fact when it is going to rain the air is more heavily charged with water vapour, and accordingly heavier, and as a result ought to make the barometer rise.—'It is chiefly in winter that hail should fall.' Indeed, since the atmosphere is colder in winter, it is clear that it is particularly in this season that raindrops should freeze and harden in passing through the atmosphere.[1]

To the extent that our interpretation of moral phenomena is founded on our presumptive knowledge of human nature, and on the supposed sameness of this nature at all times and in all places, it certainly resembles D'Alembert's 'plausible' physics. It is true that we do not always have a choice of method. In order to explain even those beliefs, customs and institutions which differ most from our own, we are very often obliged to reconstruct, as best we can, the representations and sentiments which are objectively expressed through these institutions, customs and

[1] Joseph Bertrand, *D'Alembert* (Paris, 1889), p. 17.

beliefs. But it is necessary to check and round off this procedure by use of the comparative method, that is to say the sociological method. Employed alone, it very easily leads to mistakes; we introduce our own states of mind instead of those very different ones which we have to discover. Here lies the basic defect of so many plausible but false explanations, and of so much ingenuity expended to no purpose. To look for the interpretation of myths in the impression made on us by the phenomena of nature is as hopeless as to explain polygamy by the natural inclination of man towards loose morals. The extreme cases, where the method of psychological analogy is useless, ought to put us on our guard against those instances in which it seems more satisfactory. What can it tell us about totemism?

In its present state, traditional psychology, which remains attached to the concept of 'man' in general, is open to most of the objections which this concept raises. Like the concept, it is abstract and unplaced in time. It too regards as universal whatever it finds in the subjects beneath its eyes, *hic et nunc*. It takes no account of the diversity of civilizations, nor of history; it hardly allows the vaguest idea of the progressive evolution and differentiation of the human faculties. Yet to some degree at least, the subject which it studies is a product of history. We do not know to what extent, but certainly the extent is not small. One of the most profound and original ideas of Auguste Comte, the implications of which we are far from having exhausted, is that the superior faculties of man ought to be studied in the historical development of the species. For those phenomena which should be examined above all in their relationship with their physiological antecedents and concomitants (their organic sensations, perceptions, pleasures, pains, etc.), the study of the individual may be enough; but the theory of the higher functions (imagination, language and intelligence under their various aspects) calls for the use of the sociological method.

FOR A SCIENTIFIC STUDY OF MORAL REALITY

La Morale et la science de moeurs (1903), pp. 97–100

As long as one admits the traditional conception of and distinction between theoretical ethics and practical ethics, there is no difficulty in describing their relationship. Theoretical ethics establish (either *a priori* or *a posteriori*, it little matters which at the moment) the principles which practical ethics apply. It seems that nothing could be simpler. In fact, ethical systems, almost without exception, do not consider that there is any problem here to examine. They slide very easily and without reflection from theoretical over to practical ethics. Renouvier, however, has a reservation on this point. He does not believe that the applications derived from theoretical ethics are, directly and just as they are, realizable in practice. He distinguishes between what this practice would be in 'the state of peace' (the state of a perfect society) and what it becomes in 'the state of war' (the present state of mankind). This distinction is important, for it implies that Renouvier recognizes the existence of a problem which arises the moment one passes from theory to given social practice. However Renouvier, having once made this reservation, retains the traditional conception of the relation between theory and practice in ethics. The latter is always deduced from the former. The deduction is complicated by some elements of fact which must not be neglected, but the relationship between theory and precepts remains a relationship of principles to consequences.

But if, as we believe we have shown, 'theoretical ethics' are not what they claim to be, this simple and easy relationship might itself be only an appearance. Far from the practice being deduced from the theory, it is the theory which, until now, is a sort of abstract projection of the morality practised in a given society at a given time. On the contrary then, it is the practice which is placed first, and the theory which is constrained not to run counter to this practice. Because, whatever the genius of a philosopher, he can only get his system accepted if he does not diverge too much from the common conscience of his time; whereas this conscience has no need to found itself on an abstract theory in order to impose itself with absolute authority. According to us, speculative research in ethics consists in studying just this conscience as it appears in different human societies, and in the same spirit as that in which the science of physical nature studies its object. What becomes of the relation between theory, thus understood, and practice? That is to say, supposing that this speculative research had reached a certain stage of progress, what would be the consequences for the practice?

To begin with, the old conception gave rise to an illusion which now disappears of its own accord. The relation of principle to consequence is readily confused with that of cause to effect. When we represented the practice as deduced from theoretical ethics, we were at the same time inclined to believe that philosophy, in effect, founds the practice; that with its principle it gives it its *raison d'être* and, consequently, its very reality. From now on there can be no further question of this. 'Ethics', that is to say the observable totalities of rules, prescriptions, orders and prohibitions, falls into the same category as religions, languages and laws. All these social institutions appear to us as equally natural and as interdependent. To construct or to deduce 'ethics' logically is an undertaking as irrelevant as taking it into one's head to construct or to deduce religion, language or law logically. In short, ethics are 'fundamental ideas'. It is a fact that, to every average conscience of our civilization, for example, certain kinds of action appear obligatory, others forbidden, and others neutral. There is no ground for laying down in the name of a theory the rules of ethical practice. These rules have the same sort of reality as other social facts, a reality which cannot be ignored with impunity.

Are we then reduced, so to speak, to ascertaining what have been the successive or simultaneous ethics of diverse civilizations, to establish what our own morality is, and finally to consider as rash and impractical all attempts to improve it? This is not at all a necessary conclusion.[2] Science provides us with the means to modify the physical world to our own advantage, and there is no *a priori* reason why, when it has made sufficient progress, it should not give us the same power over the social world. In fact, experience shows us that practical ethics evolve, slowly it is true, but with few interruptions. Among the very large number of causes which intervene to hasten or slow down this evolution, philosophical reflection has been, in many cases, of considerable importance. Moral practice always includes some latent contradictions which gradually and secretly make themselves felt, and reveal themselves at length, not only by strife in the field of interests but by conflict in the region of ideas. The conscious effort to resolve these contradictions has made no little contribution to moral progress.

Thus, far from having to resign ourselves to the role of passive spectators, we are constantly required to decide for or against the conservation or acceptance of this or that moral practice. To abstain is still to take sides. But how are we to decide, in the name of what principle, if our decision is to be rational? Clearly, according to the results of the positive science of social reality, which is tending to take the place of 'theoretical ethics'. The problem which arises is to establish this science, and to know how to apply it.

[2] See E. Durkheim, *De la division du travail social* (1893), 1st edition, preface, p. v; Paris, F. Alcan.

THE TYPES OF MENTALITY

Les Fonctions mentales (1910), pp. 19–21

Series of social facts are interdependent and they influence each other reciprocally. A given type of society, which has its own institutions and customs, will thus necessarily have its own mentality as well. Different social types will correspond to different mentalities, all the more since the institutions and customs themselves are basically only a certain aspect of collective representations, these representations considered objectively, so to speak. Thus one is led to think that the comparative study of different types of human societies is not separate from the comparative study of collective representations and of the connexions between these representations which dominate in these societies.

Must not similar considerations have prevailed among naturalists, when, while retaining the idea of identity of the essential functions among all living beings, or at least among all animals, they decided to acknowledge that there are fundamentally different types among them? Without doubt nutrition, respiration, secretion, and reproduction are processes which are basically invariable in whatever organism they occur. But they can occur under a collection of very different histological, anatomical, and physiological conditions. General biology took a great step forward when it recognized that to reach a greater understanding of the organism of the sponge, it did not (as Auguste Comte still believed) have to probe further the analysis of the human organism. From then on, the study of biology proper has been free of preconceived ideas about the subordination of beings one to another, with reservations made on the possibility of original common forms preceding the divergence of types.

Equally, there are some characteristics common to all human societies which distinguish them from animal societies; there is language spoken, traditions passed on, and institutions maintained. As a result their superior mental operations have everywhere a basis which cannot but be the same. Granted this point, human societies, like organisms, can present structures radically different one from another, and consequently corresponding differences in their higher mental operations. We must therefore refrain from first reducing mental operations to a single type, whatever the societies considered, and from explaining all collective representations by a psychological and logical machinery which is always the same. If it is true that there exist human societies which, in their structure, differ among themselves in the same way as animals without vertebrae differ from those with vertebrae, the comparative study of varying types of collective mentality is no less indispensable to the science of man than are comparative anatomy and physiology to biology.

Is it necessary to say that this comparative study, thus broadly conceived, presents at the moment some insurmountable difficulties? In the present state of sociology, one would not dream of undertaking it. The determination of types of mentality is as difficult as that of types of society, and for the same reasons. What I am going to attempt here, as an essay or introduction, is the preliminary study of the most general laws obeyed by collective representations in simpler societies, and more especially in the simplest societies we know. I will endeavour to set up, if not a type, at least a collection of characteristics common to a group of neighbouring types, and thus to define the essential traits of the mentality peculiar to simpler societies.

In order better to sort out these traits, I will compare this mentality with ours, that is to say with that of societies born of the Mediterranean civilization, where rationalist philosophy and positive science developed. For a first outline of a comparative study, there is an obvious advantage in choosing the two mental types available for our investigation between which the distance is *greatest*. It is between them that the essential differences will be more marked, and accordingly will have less chance of escaping our notice. Again, in starting with these it will be easier afterwards to approach the study of intermediary or transitional forms.

Even with these restrictions, the attempt will doubtless appear too ambitious, and of doubtful success. It remains unfinished, it probably asks more questions than it answers, it smoothes down one problem and leaves a greater one unsolved. I am aware of this, but in the analysis of so obscure a mentality I have thought it preferable to confine myself to what I saw clearly. Then again, with regard to the mentality peculiar to our society, which should serve me simply as a basis for comparison, I shall consider it well enough defined in the works of philosophers, logicians, and psychologists, both ancient and modern, without prejudging how a future sociological analysis could modify the results obtained by them up until now. The proper object of my researches thus remains the study, through the collective representations of simpler societies, of the mental processes which order them.

HOW TO APPROACH THE STUDY OF PRIMITIVE PEOPLES

La Mentalité primitive (1922), pp. 15–16

Instead of imagining ourselves in the place of the primitive people we are studying, and making them think as we would think if we were in their place, which can only lead to hypotheses at the very most probable and almost always wrong, let us try, on the contrary, to guard against our own mental habits, and endeavour to discover those of primitive peoples by the analysis of their collective representations and the connexions between them.

As long as one thinks that their mind is oriented like ours, that it reacts as ours does to the impressions which it receives, one also implicitly concedes that it *must* reflect and reason on the phenomena and beings of the given world as ours does. But one establishes that in fact it neither reflects nor reasons in this way. In order to explain this apparent anomaly, one then has recourse to a certain number of hypotheses—the laziness and feebleness of the primitive mind, confusion, infantile ignorance, stupidity, etc. —which do not take adequate account of the facts.

Let us abandon this postulate and attempt, without any preconceived ideas, the objective study of primitive mentality, such as it appears in the institutions of simpler societies or in the collective representations whence these institutions arise. From then on, the mental activity of primitive peoples will no longer be interpreted in advance as a rudimentary form of ours, as infantile and almost pathological. On the contrary, it will appear normal under the conditions where it is practised, and complex and developed in its own way. By ceasing to relate it to a type which is not its own, and by seeking to determine the mechanism solely according to its actual manifestations, we can hope not to misrepresent it in our description and our analysis.

THE COLLECTIVE REPRESENTATIONS OF PRIMITIVE PEOPLES

Les Fonctions mentales (1910), pp. 27–30

Before undertaking research into the most general laws which govern the collective representations of simpler societies, perhaps it will not be useless to determine briefly the essential features of these representations, and thus prevent some almost inevitable misunderstandings. The terminology used in the analysis of mental functions is suited to such functions as philosophers, psychologists and logicians have established and defined in our society. As long as one accepts that these functions are identical in all human societies, there is no difficulty: the same terminology can be used everywhere, with the reservation that 'savages' have the mentality of children rather than of adults. But, if one rejects this postulate—and we have the strongest reasons to regard it as poorly founded—then the terms, divisions and classifications which are used to analyse our mental operations are no longer suitable for the workings which differ from them, and become, on the contrary, a source of confusion and error. For the study of the mentality of primitive peoples, which is new, perhaps it is necessary to have a new terminology. At least it will be vital to specify the new sense which a certain number of accepted terms ought to take, when one applies them to an object different from that previously designated.

This is the case, for example, with the term 'collective representations'.

In the current language of psychology, which classifies facts as emotional, motivational, and intellectual, 'representation' is placed in this last category. One understands by it a fact of cognizance, inasmuch as the mind simply has the image or the idea of an object. It is not denied that, in actual mental life, every representation more or less affects the inclinations, and tends to produce or to inhibit some action. But, by an abstraction which in a large number of cases is not extreme, we ignore these elements of the representation, and retain only its essential relationship with the object which it makes known. The representation is, *par excellence*, an intellectual or cognitive phenomenon.

The collective representations of primitive peoples should not be understood thus. Their mental activity is too undifferentiated for it to be possible to consider the ideas or images of objects by themselves, independently of the sentiments, emotions and passions which evoke or are evoked by these ideas and images. Just because our mental activity is more differentiated, and also because the analysis of its operations is familiar to us, it is very difficult for us to appreciate, by an effort of imagination, more complex states where the emotional and motivational elements are *integral parts* of representations. It seems to us that these states are not truly representations, and indeed, in order to keep this term we must change its meaning. What must be understood by this form of mental activity among primitive peoples is not a pure or almost pure intellectual or cognitive phenomenon, but a more complex phenomenon in which what for us is really 'representation' is still mixed with other elements of an emotional or motivational character, coloured and pervaded by them, and, in consequence, implying a different attitude with regard to the objects represented.

Moreover, these collective representations are very often acquired by the individual in circumstances likely to make the deepest impression on his feelings. This is particularly true of those which are transmitted to him at the moment when he becomes a man, a conscious member of his social group, when initiation ceremonies give him rebirth, and when secrets are revealed to him on which the very life of his group depends, sometimes in the midst of tortures which put his nerves to the severest tests. It would be difficult to exaggerate the intensity of the emotional force of these representations. The object is not simply apprehended by the mind in the form of an idea or image; according to the case, fear, hope, religious awe, the need and burning desire to blend in a common essence, and the passionate appeal to a protecting power are the heart of these representations, and make them at one and the same time cherished, formidable, and truly *sacred* to those who have been initiated. Add to this the ceremonies in which these representations are periodically put into action, so to speak, the well-known effect of the contagion of emotions when watching the actions which express them, the nervous over-excitement produced by excessive tiredness, the dances, the phenomena of ecstasy and possession, everything in fact which tends to revive and aggravate the emotional nature of these collective representations. Then, in the period between these ceremonies, when the object of one of these representations leaps to the consciousness of the 'primitive man', even if at this moment he is alone and quiet, this object will never appear to him in the form of a colourless and neutral image. A wave of emotion will immediately sweep over him, doubtless less violent than during the ceremonies, but strong enough for the cognitive aspect almost to disappear beneath the feelings which enfold him. To a lesser degree other collective representations have the same characteristics, those, for example, which are transmitted from generation to generation by myths and stories, and those which govern the customs and usages which appear least important. For if these usages are respected and enforced, it is because the collective representations concerning them are imperative, and quite different from purely intellectual phenomena.

The collective representations of primitive peoples thus differ profoundly from our ideas and concepts; they are in no way equivalent. On one hand, as we shall soon see, they do not possess a logical nature. On the other hand, not being pure representations, in the proper sense of the word, they express, or rather imply, not only that primitive man actually has an image of the object and believes that it is real, but also that he hopes or fears for something from it, that a certain action should emanate from it or be exerted on it. This is an influence, a virtue, an occult power, varying according to the objects and to the circumstances, but which always remains real for primitive man, and forms an integral part of his representation. In order to designate by one word this general property of collective representations, which hold so large a place in the mental activity of simpler societies, I will say that this mental activity is *mystical*. I will use this term, for lack of a better, not with allusion to the religious mysticism of our own societies, which is something quite different, but in the narrowly defined sense in which 'mystical' is used of the belief in forces, influences, and actions, imperceptible to the senses but nonetheless real.

Les Fonctions mentales (1910), pp. 68–70

If the collective representations of primitive peoples differ from ours through their essentially mystical character, if their mentality, as I have tried to show, is oriented differently from ours, we must admit that neither are the representations linked in their mind as they are in ours. Must we infer from this that these representations obey a logic other than that which we understand? This would be saying too much, and the hypothesis would go beyond what the facts permit us to affirm. There is no proof that the connexions between collective representations must depend solely on laws which have a logical character. Moreover, the idea of a logic other than that of our understanding would be for us only a negative and empty concept. But in fact we can at least try to apprehend how the representations are connected in the mentality of primitive peoples. We understand their languages, we strike bargains with them, and we manage to interpret their institutions and their beliefs; there is thus a possible bridge, a practicable communication between their mentality and ours.

With these reservations, the mentalities are, nevertheless, different. The disparity becomes the more apparent the more prolonged the comparative study, and as documents have permitted it to be further extended. The explorer who rapidly passes through a society of the simpler sort has not the time to examine this question. He hardly ever even thinks of asking it. By turns he records the remarkable permanence of certain traits of human nature revealed in the most diverse conditions, and expresses his surprise in the presence of manners of thought and action whose origin and reason escape him. He leaves to the reader the trouble of finding out how to reconcile these successive impressions, or else he limits himself to general 'explanations' furnished by traditional psychology and logic, if he has some smattering of them.

But when we listen to observers who have lived for a longer time among primitive people, and particularly those who have made an effort to understand their manner of feeling and thinking, we hear a very different story. Whether it is a matter of the North American Indians (of whom Cushing and Major Powell tell us), of the Negroes of the French Congo (after Miss Kingsley), or the Maoris of New Zealand (following Elsdon Best), or any other 'primitive' society whatever, never, we are told, can a 'civilized man' feel sure of seeing his thought follow exactly the same step as that of primitive man, nor of retracing the route by which it has passed. 'The mentality of the Maori' says Elsdon Best for example, 'is of an intensly mystical nature. . . . We hear of many singular theories anent Maori beliefs and Maori thought, but the truth is that we do not understand either, and, what is more, we never shall. We shall never know the inwardness of the native mind. For that would mean retracing our steps for many centuries . . . to the time when we also possessed the mind of primitive man. And the gates have long closed on that hidden road.'[3]

Cushing acquired a sort of mental naturalization among the Zuñi. Not content with living among them and like them for

[3] Elsdon Best, 'Maori Medical Lore', *Journal of the Polynesian Society*, XIII (1904), p. 219.

many years, he had himself initiated and adopted by their religious leaders, and affiliated to their secret societies; and in their sacred ceremonies, he had, like the priests, his own role which he performed. But the all too few works of his which have been published give us precisely the feeling of a form of mental activity to which our mind will never exactly conform. Our intellectual habits are too far from those of the Zuñi. Our language (without which we can represent nothing, nor can we reason) involves categories which do not coincide with theirs. Lastly and above all, the surrounding social reality, of which the collective representations, and even up to a certain point, the language, are functions, differs too much from our own environment.

Thus the mentality of simpler societies is doubtless not as impenetrable as it would be if it obeyed a logic different from ours, but it is nonetheless not entirely intelligible to us. We are led to think that it does not exclusively obey the laws of *our* logic, nor perhaps laws which are all by nature logical. Analysis of the most characteristic facts will be able to shed some light on this point for us.

THE LAW OF PARTICIPATION AND THE PRELOGICAL

Les Fonctions mentales (1910), pp. 76–80

The minds of primitive people are simply not ready to receive and are not disposed to submit passively to the impression of what we call experience and the sequence of events. On the contrary, these minds are occupied in advance by a large number of collective representations, as a result of which, things, whatever they may be—living beings, inanimate objects, or articles manufactured by man—only appear to them charged with mystical properties. Consequently, these minds, while very often indifferent to objective relationships, are above all attentive to mystical connexions, actual or virtual. These premoulded connexions do not derive their origin from present experience, and against them experience can do nothing.

Let us then no longer try to account for these connexions either by the feebleness of primitive people's minds or by the association of ideas, or by a naive use of the principle of causality, or by the fallacy *post hoc, ergo propter hoc*; in brief, to want to reduce their mental activity to an inferior form of our own. Let us rather consider these connexions in themselves, and see if they do not depend on a general law, a common foundation for these mystical relationships which the mentality of primitive people so often sees between beings and objects. Now there is an element which is never absent in these relationships. Under various forms and degrees, all imply a 'participation' between the beings or the objects linked in a collective representation. This is why, for want of a better term, I shall call the appropriate principle of the 'primitive' mentality which governs the connexions and the preconnexions of these representations, the *law of participation*.

It would have been difficult, before now, to give an abstract statement of this law. It will be adequately defined in the course of this chapter, although what it is concerned to express can only penetrate the ordinary framework of our thought with great difficulty. However, in the absence of a satisfying formula, one can attempt an approximation. I would say that, in the collective representations of the primitive mentality, objects, beings and phenomena can, in a way incomprehensible to us, be at one and the same time themselves and something other than themselves. In a fashion no less incomprehensible, they emit and receive mystical forces, properties, qualities and actions which are felt outside themselves, without them ceasing to be where they are.

In other words, for this mentality, the opposition between one and many, the same and another, etc., does not impose the necessity to affirm one of the terms if one denies the other, and vice-versa. This is of only secondary interest. Sometimes it is perceived, but often it is not. Often it is obscured by a mystical community of essence between beings which nevertheless could never be confused in our thought without absurdity. For example, 'The Trumai [a tribe of North Brazil] say that they are aquatic animals. The Bororo [a neighbouring tribe] claim to be red arara (parrots).' This does not simply mean that after death they become parrots, no more than that parrots are transformed Bororo and ought to be treated as such. It means something completely different. 'The Bororo,' says von den Steinen, who was not willing to believe it but who had to give in to their explicit affirmations, 'give unemotionally to understand that they *are actually* parrots, exactly as if a caterpillar were to say that it was a butterfly.'[4] It is not a name which they give themselves, nor is it some kinship which they claim. What they wish to convey is an essential

[4] K. von den Steinen, *Unter den Naturvölkern Zentralbräsiliens* (1894), pp. 305–6.

identity. That they are at the same time the human beings which they are, and birds with red plumage, Von den Steinen judges to be inconceivable. However, for a mentality ruled by the law of participation, this presents no difficulty. All societies of totemic form admit of collective representations of the same type, which imply a similar identity between the individuals of a totemic group and their totem.

In the same way, from a dynamic point of view, the creation of beings and phenomena, and the occurrence of such or such an event, result from a mystical influence which is communicated, under conditions themselves mystical, from one object or being to another. They depend on a participation which is represented in very diverse forms: contact, transference, sympathy, telekinesis, etc. In a large number of societies of the simpler type, the abundance of game, fish, or fruit, and the regularity of the seasons and the rains, are associated with the carrying out of certain ceremonies by specified people, or with the presence or well-being of a sacred person who possesses a special mystical quality. Or yet again, the newborn child suffers the consequences of everything his father does, eats, etc. The Indian, hunting or at war, is lucky or unlucky, depending on whether his wife back at the camp does or does not abstain from certain foods or actions. Relationships of this type are innumerable in collective representations, while what we call the natural relations of causality between events pass unnoticed, or have only minimal importance. It is the mystical participations which occupy first place, and often the whole place.

This is why the mentality of primitive peoples can be called *prelogical* just as fairly as *mystical.* Here there are two aspects of one fundamental property, rather than two distinct characteristics. This mentality, if one considers more especially the contents of the representations, will be called mystical—and if one is concerned rather with the connexions, prelogical. By prelogical one must not understand that this mentality constitutes a sort of stage in time before the appearance of logical thought. Have there ever existed groups of human or prehuman beings whose collective representations did not yet obey logical laws? We do not know; in any case, it is very unlikely. At least, the mentality of societies of the simpler type, which I call *prelogical*, through lack of a better name, does not present this character at all. It is not *antilogical*; no more is it *alogical*. In calling it prelogical, I only want to say that unlike our thought, it does not have to abstain from contradiction. It obeys firstly the law of participation. Thus directed, it does not take gratuitous pleasure in contradiction (which would habitually make it absurd for us), but neither does it consider avoiding it. Mostly it is indifferent to it, and this is why it is so difficult to follow.

As has been said, these characteristics only apply to collective representations and their connexions. A primitive man, considered as an individual, in so far as he thinks and acts independently of these collective representations, if that is possible, will usually feel, judge, and behave in the way we would expect. The inferences which he will form will be just those which would seem reasonable to us in the given circumstances. If, for example, he has shot two pieces of game, and he can find only one to pick up, he will wonder what has become of the other and look for it. If he is caught in the rain and dislikes it, he will seek shelter. If he meets a savage animal, he will plan how to escape from it, etc. Although on occasions of this sort, primitive men will reason like us and will adhere to behaviour similar to ours (as, in the simplest cases, the most intelligent animals can do), it does not follow that their mental activity always obeys the same laws as ours. In fact, in so far as it is collective, it has laws which are peculiarly its own, of which the first and the most general is the law of participation.

The very material on which this mental activity is exercised has already come under the influence of the law of participation. For collective representations are totally different from our concepts. The latter, the stuff of our logical operations, already result, as one knows, from earlier operations of the same type. The simple statement of a general abstract term, such as man, animal, or organism, to all intents and purposes contains a large number of judgements which imply definite relationships between many concepts. But the collective representations of primitive peoples are not, like our concepts, the result of an intellectual effort, properly so-called. They contain, as integral parts, emotional and motivational elements, and above all, instead of conceptual inclusions and exclusions they involve participations, more or less well defined but in general vividly felt.

LANGUAGE AND NUMERATION

Les Fonctions mentales (1910), pp. 152–5

Perhaps the most salient characteristic of the majority of the languages of the North American Indians is the care which they take in expressing concrete details which our languages leave implied or unexpressed. 'A *Ponka* Indian, in saying that a man killed a rabbit, would have to say the man, he, one, animate, standing, in the nominative case, purposely killed, by shooting an arrow, the rabbit, he, the one, animate, sitting in the objective case; for the form of a verb to kill would have to be selected, and the verb changes its form by inflection and incorporated particles to denote person, number, and gender as animate or inanimate, and gender as standing, sitting, or lying, and case; and the form of the verb would also express whether the killing was done accidentally or purposely, and whether it was by shooting . . . and, if by shooting, whether by bow and arrow, or with a gun'.[5] In the language of the Cherokee also, 'instead of the vague expression *we*, there are distinct modifications meaning respectively, 'I and thou', 'I and ye', 'I and ye two', 'I and he', 'I and they', 'I and they two'; also united with the dual, 'we two and thou', 'we two and ye', etc.—and in the plural. 'I, thou and he or they'; 'I, ye and he or they'; etc., etc. In the simple conjugation of the present, of the indicative, including the pronouns in the nominative and oblique cases, there are not less than seventy

[5] J. W. Powell, 'On the evolution of language', *Ethnology Bureau Report*, I (1879–80), p. 16.

distinct forms . . . other nice distinctions, in reference to the verb, the various forms of which denote, whether the object be animate or inanimate; whether or not the person spoken of, either as agent or object, is expected to hear what is said; and, in regard to the dual and plural numbers, whether the action terminates upon the several objects collectively, as if it were one object, or upon each individual considered separately.'[6]

Thus these languages, like ours, know the category of number; but they do not express it in the same way. We oppose the plural to the singular; a subject or object is either singular or plural. This mental habit involves a familiar and rapid use of abstraction, that is to say of logical thought and its working stock. The prelogical mentality does not proceed thus. 'To the observing mind of the primeval Klamath Indian' writes Gatschet in his excellent grammar of the Klamath language, 'the fact that sundry things were done repeatedly, at different times, or that the same thing was done severally by distinct persons, appeared much more important than the pure idea of plurality, as we have it in our own language.'[7] The Klamath language does not have the plural but distributive reduplication serves instead. 'Wherever this form is indicating plurality it does so only because the idea of severalty happens to coincide with that of plurality . . .

'Thus nép means *hands* as well as *hand*, *the hand*, *a hand*, but its distributive form nénap means each of the two hands or the hand of each person when considered as a separate individual. Ktchō'l signifies *star*, *the star*, *a star*, *the stars*, *constellation* or *constellations*, but d.Ktchóktchōl means *each star* or *every star* or *constellation* considered separately . . . Pádsha î: *you became blind of one eye*; d. papádsha î: *you are totally blind*, *you lost the use of your eyes*.'[8]

Is this to say that the Klamath language does not express the

[6] Gallatin, *Transactions of the American Ethnological Society*, II (1848), pp. cxxx–cxxxi.

[7] A. S. Gatschet, 'Ethnographic Sketch of the Klamath People', *Contributions to North American Ethnology*, II (1890), p. 419.

[8] Ibid., pp. 262–3.

plural? Yes indeed; but it manages it by means of various methods. For example, it indicates that the subject of the phrase is in the plural thus:

'a. . . . is indicated analytically by adding to the noun, a numeral or an indefinite pronoun (some, many, all, few).

b. . . . is shown by the noun being a collective, or one of the substantives designating persons, which possess a form for the real plural.

c. The large majority of substantives have no real plural, their plurality is indicated in the intransitive verbs . . . by the distributive form of the verb, and in a few transitive verbs . . . by a special form which has also a distributive function.

d. When there are but two, three, or, at the utmost, four subjects to certain intransitive verbs, the dual form of the latter will be used.' [9]

To judge by this example, which is not at all exceptional, if the prelogical mentality originally does not use the plural form, it is because that form is not explicit enough, and does not specify the particular modalities of the plural. This mentality needs to express whether it is concerned with two or three, few or many subjects or objects, and whether they are together or separate. Likewise, as we will see below, it will not possess a general term for 'tree', or for 'fish', but special terms for each variety of tree or fish. Thus it will have ways of expressing, not just the plural pure and simple, but diverse varieties of the plural. In general, this trait will be even more marked when we come to consider the languages spoken in social groups where the prelogical mentality predominates more.

[9] Ibid., pp. 578–9.

MEMORY

Les Fonctions mentales (1910), pp. 116–18

In the first place, the memory plays a more important part in the prelogical mentality than in our mental life, where certain functions which it used to perform have been taken from it and have changed. Our store of social thought is transmitted condensed in a hierarchy of concepts which are coordinated with and subordinated to each other. In simpler societies, it consists of an often immense number of complex and voluminous collective representations; it is thus transmitted almost solely by memory. In the whole course of life, whether sacred or profane things are concerned, a sign which, without us having to will it, arouses in us the exercise of logic, awakens in primitive man a complex and often mystical recollection which governs his action. And this very memory has a special tonality which distinguishes it from ours. The constant use of logical operations which abstract concepts entail, the, as it were, natural use of languages which rests on this operation, disposes our memory to retain by preference the relationships which have a preponderant importance from an objective and logical viewpoint. In the prelogical mentality, memory has a very different aspect and tendencies because its content is different. It is, at one and the same time, very reliable and very emotional. It reconstructs the complex collective representations with great richness of detail, and always in the order in which they are linked traditionally to each other, according to mainly mystical relationships. Thus while compensating to a certain degree for logical functions, it also exercises their prerogatives to the same degree. For example, a representation unavoidably evoked through the memory as a sequel to another often has the quality of a conclusion. This is why, as we will see, a sign is almost always taken for a cause.

The preconnexions, the preperceptions and the prerationalizations which take up so much room in the mentality of simpler societies involve no logical activity at all, and are simply entrusted to the memory. Thus we must expect to see the memory highly developed among primitive peoples. This, in fact, is what observers tell us. But since they assume, without thinking about it, that it has just the same functions there as in our societies, they are surprised and disconcerted by it. It seems to them that it does something quite extraordinary when it is simply working normally. 'In many respects their memory is phenomenal,' say Spencer and Gillen in speaking of the Australians. 'Not only does the native know the track of every beast and bird, but after examining any burrow he will at once, from the direction in which the last track runs, tell you whether the animal is at home or not . . . Strange as it may sound . . . the native will recognize the footprint of every individual of his acquaintance.' [10]

[10] Spencer & Gillen, *The Native Tribes of Central Australia* (1899), pp. 25–6, p. 483.

CAUSALITY

La Mentalité primitive (1922), pp. 17–18

In the presence of something which interests, troubles, or frightens it, the mind of primitive man does not follow the same course as ours. It goes off at once in a different direction.

We have a permanent sense of intellectual security so well founded that we do not see how it could be shaken; for, even supposing the sudden appearance of a completely mysterious phenomenon whose causes, at first, entirely escape us, we will nonetheless be persuaded that our ignorance is only temporary, that these causes exist and that sooner or later they may be determined. Thus nature, in the midst of which we live, is, so to speak, intellectualized in advance. It has order and reason like the mind which conceives it and moves in it. Our daily activity, even in its humblest details, involves a quiet and perfect confidence in the invariability of natural laws.

Very different is the attitude of the mind of primitive man. The nature in which he lives appears to him under a very different guise. There all objects and beings are involved in a network of mystical participations and exclusions, and it is these which form its structure and order. Consequently it is these which will first force themselves on his attention and they alone will hold it. If he is interested by a phenomenon, and if he does not merely perceive it, passively and without reaction so to speak, he will immediately think, as by a sort of mental reflex, of an occult and invisible power of which the phenomenon is the manifestation. 'The viewpoint of the native African mind,' says Nassau, 'in all unusual occurrences, is that of witchcraft. Without looking for an explanation in what civilization would call *natural* causes, his thought turns at once to the supernatural. Indeed, the supernatural is so constant a factor in his life, that to him it furnishes explanation of events as prompt and reasonable as our reference to the recognized forces of nature.'[11] Likewise observes the Reverend John Philip with reference to the 'superstitions of the Bechuana': 'Everything in a state of ignorance [that is to say before receiving instruction from the missionaries], which is not known, and which is involved in mystery [of which simple perception is not enough to provide a reason], is the object of superstitious veneration, where second causes are unknown, and invisible agency is substituted in their places.'[12]

La Mentalité primitive (1922), p. 20

For a mentality so oriented and totally preoccupied with mystical preconnexions, what we call a cause or what for us makes sense of whatever happens, at the very most could only be a chance, or better still, an instrument in the service of occult forces. The occasion could have been otherwise or the instrument different, but the event would have happened all the same. It was enough that the occult force should have really come into action without being stopped by a superior force of the same type.

La Mentalité primitive (1922), pp. 510–12

Primitive mentality, like ours, worries about the causes of what happens, but it does not seek them in the same way. It exists in a world where innumerable occult powers, everywhere present, are

[11] R. H. Nassau, *Fetichism in West Africa* (1904), p. 277

[12] J. Philip, *Researches in South Africa*, II (1828), pp. 116–17.

always active or ready to act. As we have seen in the first part of this book, every happening that is a little unusual is taken immediately as a manifestation of one or many of them. Does the rain come when the fields are greatly in need of water? It is because the ancestors and the spirits of the place are satisfied, and thus bear witness of their good will. If the persisting drought burns the crops, and causes the beasts to perish, has a taboo perhaps been violated? Or perhaps an ancestor feels offended, and his anger must be appeased. Likewise, an enterprise will never succeed without the help of the invisible powers. No one will go hunting or fishing, no one will go to war, no one will start to cultivate a field or build a house, if favourable omens have not appeared, if the mystical protectors of the social group have not expressly promised their help, if the very animals one wishes to catch do not consent, if the equipment has not been consecrated and invested with magical qualities, etc. In short, the visible world and the invisible world form one, and the events of the visible world depend at each instance on the powers of the other. This accounts for the place which dreams, omens, divination in a thousand different forms, sacrifices, incantations, ritual ceremonies, and magic hold in the life of primitive man. This accounts for their habit of neglecting what we call secondary causes, and of giving all their attention to the mystical cause as the only truly efficient one. A man succumbs to an organic illness, to a snake bite, he is crushed by a falling tree, eaten by a tiger or a crocodile, but for the primitive mentality it is not the sickness, nor the snake, nor the tree, nor the tiger, nor the crocodile which has killed him. If he perished, it is without doubt because a sorcerer had 'doomed' and 'delivered' him. The fatal tree or animal has been only an instrument. In the absence of one, the other would have done the same job. They were, so to speak, interchangeable, at the will of the invisible power which employed them.

For minds so oriented, there is no purely physical fact. Thus no question concerning the phenomena of nature appears to them in the same way as it does to us. When we wish to explain such a phenomenon, we look in the same series of phenomena for the necessary and sufficient conditions. If we manage to determine them, we do not ask for more. Knowledge of the law is enough for us. The attitude of primitive man is completely different. He has perhaps noticed the constant antecedents of the fact which concerns him, and, in his behaviour, takes the greatest account of these observations. But he will always see the real cause in the world of invisible powers, beyond what we call nature, in the 'metaphysical' in the true sense of the word. In brief, our problems are not theirs, and their problems are foreign to us. This is why to wonder what solution he would give to one of ours, to imagine it and to claim to draw conclusions from it which would explain such or such a primitive institution, is to enter a blind-alley.

MISONEISM

La Mentalité primitive (1922), pp. 445–6

Having tried to analyse the primitive mentality, at least in the essential characteristics of its structure and mechanism, it would be of great interest to examine how it develops, and according to what laws. Unfortunately, the necessary elements for a task of this sort are still lacking. With very rare exceptions, simpler societies have no history. Their myths, so instructive in other ways, cannot take its place. The little we know with accuracy about their institutions and their languages allows us only to make arbitrary hypotheses.

At present, however, it is possible to make a general comment, founded on the evidence of a large number of observers. Simple societies, in general, show hostility towards everything which comes from outside, at least so long as it is not a neighbouring tribe similar to themselves, of the same blood, customs and institutions, and with whom they might live on good terms. From the stranger, properly so called, they neither borrow nor accept anything. Changes, even when incontestably progressive, have to be imposed on them, for if they are free to accept or reject them their choice is not in doubt. They are formed like closed systems where everything which enters risks triggering off a process of decomposition. They are like organisms capable of strong and lengthy life as long as the environment varies little, but which, if some new elements burst in, rapidly degenerate and die.

La Mentalité primitive (1922), pp. 452–3

If it is a matter of abandoning a traditional custom, or of deliberately adopting a previously unknown practice, the resistance is as lively as it is stubborn. Observers, and above all missionaries, have clearly seen the reason why. 'The New Guinea man,' says Newton, 'is intensely conservative, and he does what his father and grandfather and great-grandfather did: what was good enough for them is good enough for him, as the man who was building a canoe in Wedau rejected with scorn the suggestion to build a big comfortable platform in the centre as the Boianai people do, instead of the little skimpy things at each end the Wedau affect—'No, it is not our way' (and perhaps the Boianai people might object to infringment of their patent rights).' [13]

The same missionary recounts that the natives, at a certain large feast, used to sacrifice pigs in the cruellest and slowest manner, and that they had been persuaded henceforth to kill the victims more quickly and humanely. The feast came round, and 'very early in the morning the killing of the pigs began, and towards the end some of the old people got anxious at the awful breach of custom . . . and a deputation came to say [to the missionaries] they must kill one pig in their own way so that the mango trees might hear the squeals, otherwise they would not bear fruit.' [14]

[13] H. Newton, *In far New Guinea* (1914), pp. 125–6.
[14] Ibid., p. 154.

CONFUSION BETWEEN THE MATERIAL AND THE SPIRITUAL

L'Âme primitive (1927), 131–132

The opposition between matter and spirit with which we are so familiar, to the point that it seems almost natural to us, does not exist in the primitive mentality. Or, at least, the latter interprets it differently from us. For the primitive mentality there is neither matter nor body which does not give forth some mystical force which we would call spiritual. Neither is there a spiritual reality which is not a complete being, that is to say something concrete, with the form of a body, even if it is invisible, intangible, and with neither consistency nor density. Here is some evidence taken from among numerous examples. '. . . the African does not believe in anything being soulless, he regards even matter itself as a form of soul, low, because not lively, a thing other spirit forms use as they please—practically as the cloth of the spirit that uses it. This conception is, as far as I know, constant in both Negro and Bantu.'[15]—In Canada, 'The Ten'a do not conceive the spirits as really spiritual, or immaterial, substances. For them, the spirits have a sort of subtle body, a kind of aerial fluid, so to speak, capable of endless transformations, moving from place to place almost instantaneously, rendering itself visible and invisible at will, penetrating into other bodies, and passing through them as though they were no obstacles, in short, possessed

[15] M. Kingsley, *West African studies* (1899), p. 199.

of the qualities proper to real spirits. But the conception of a real spiritual substance is beyond Ten'a intelligence.' [16]

It is to Elsdon Best that we owe, on this point, the clearest and most comprehensive formulation: '... confusion is caused in our minds by the native terms denoting both material representations of immaterial qualities and immaterial representations of material objects.' [17] Representations, let us add, which are extremely difficult, if not impossible, for minds fashioned like ours to reconstitute. Therefore, what indication is there that those of the body, of the soul and of their relationships should be, I do not say similar, but only comparable, between primitive peoples and us?

[16] Julius Jetté, On the superstitions of the Ten'a Indians, *Anthropos* VI (1911), p. 97.

[17] Elsdon Best, *The Maori* I (1924), p. 299.

APPURTENANCES

L'Âme primitive (1927), pp. 132–4

All of us believe that we know exactly how our individual personality is formed, and where its boundaries come. I am my feelings, my thoughts, my memories. My head, my arms, my legs, my internal organs, etc., are also me. Everything else which I perceive is not me. My individuality is thus grasped by my consciousness and circumscribed by the surface of my body, and I believe that that of my neighbour is exactly like mine.

Among primitive peoples also, each individual ascribes to himself his states of consciousness, his limbs, and his organs. Certain languages even express this fact by personal pronouns suffixed to the substantives which designate these parts of the individual. But this suffixing extends further, and it is applied also to the names of objects which are in intimate relationship with the individual, and which form, so to speak, part of him. In effect, in the representations of primitive peoples, as has often been noted, the individuality of each person does not stop at the periphery of his person. Its boundaries are vague, ill-determined, and even variable, depending on how much or little of the mystical force or *mana* individuals possess.

In the first place the primitive mentality includes, along with the body itself, whatever grows on it and whatever comes out of it, secretions and excretions: head and body hair, nails, tears, urine, excrement, semen, sweat, etc. It is enough to recall the celebrated articles in *Globus* in which K. Th. Preuss showed that magical practices exercised on these products of the body act on the person himself of whom they are integral parts.[18] This explains the extreme care which, in a large number of societies, everyone takes to avoid his hair, or nail-parings, or excrement, etc., from falling into the hands of a third party, who might have wicked intentions. To dispose of one of these is to dispose of one's life. The body hair, secretions, etc., of the individual are him in the same sense that his feet, hands, heart and head are. They 'belong' to him in the fullest sense of the word. Henceforth I will refer to these things as his 'appurtenances'.

To these parts of the individuality must be added the imprints which the body leaves on a seat or on the ground, and footprints in particular. Thus, in a popular story from the Island of Kiwai, 'He was out of reach when the people got to know of his visit, and the only thing they could do was to shoot off their arrows into his foottracks, thus trying to hurt him.'[19] In another part of New Guinea, a rainmaker was successful and, 'On his return, the hero was met at the village with loud beating of drums, the mothers taking their babies and setting them down in his foot-prints, thinking perhaps that their little bodies might gather up some of the knowledge of this marvellous man.'[20]

L'Âme primitive (1927), pp. 135–6

The remains of a man's food also belong, as we know, to the number of his appurtenances. We can easily understand that there is an identity of substance established between a man and what he eats; he becomes, he is what he eats and assimilates. This participation, according to the primitive mentality, extends to the remains; the unconsumed portion of the food is as valid as the other.

[18] K. Th. Preuss, Der Ursprung der Religion und Kunst, *Globus* (1903), LXXXVI.

[19] G. Landtman, *The Folk-tales of the Kiwai Papuans* (1917), p. 418.

[20] *Annual Report*, *Papua* (South-Eastern Division) (1910), p. 78.

L'Âme primitive (1927), p. 137

One can say as much, odd though it may appear, about the clothes which have been worn by their owner, and have been soaked in his sweat. Thus on the Island of Kiwai, 'One day the girls on their way home from fishing came to Báidam's abode and picked up the leaves which he had used when dancing. They stuck them inside their grass-petticoats and went home to sleep, and from Báidam's "smell" they all became pregnant.'[21] A similar belief has been recorded in Madagascar. 'The father's lamba ought not to be carried by his daughter; likewise, the sister should not carry her brother's lamba.'[22] Again among the Baghirmi, 'The Kozzam are attached to a larger tribe called the Hémat. The legend about their origin tells that they are descended from an Arab Al Ouémit who left Mecca accompanied by his pubescent but still virgin daughter. The girl no longer having an apron, her father gave her his trousers to hide her nakedness. Some time later, the virgin realized that she was pregnant as a result of this act alone. She gave birth to a son, which she and her father abandoned on a mountain.[23]

L'Âme primitive (1927), pp. 141–2

In certain societies, one also reckons among the number of appurtenances the things which an individual owns, above all when it is a matter of objects which he himself has produced or made. These objects are inseparable from his person; they form part of him, they are himself. Property, in these cases, according to the comment of Dr. Thurnwald, should be called 'personal' rather than 'individual'. 'Work and its products' he says, 'are regarded,

[21] G. Landtman, *The Folk-tales of the Kiwai Papuans* (1917), p. 268.

[22] R. Decary, Notes ethnographiquees sur les populations du district de Maromandia, *Revue d'ethnographie et des traditions populaires*, V (1924), p. 355.

[23] Devallée, Le Baghirmi, *Recherches congolaises*, VII (1925), p. 20.

in their nature as the highest degree of personal manifestation, as indissolubly linked to their author, like an 'appurtenance' (*Zubehör*). This is why such things ought to disappear at the same time as him. One burns them when he dies.' [24] This feeling is almost universal. It results in the destruction of a man's belongings when he is no more; it results in regarding any attempt on such objects as the most serious of injuries, as if their owner were alive. '. . . the natives are absurdly sensitive to threats of *burning* anything belonging to themselves. There is no surer way of drawing down this anger than to hint at such a thing as the *burning* of a canoe, a hut, or even a garment. *To chop the property* of another is regarded as symbolical of an intention to *chop his person*.' [25]

[24] R. Thurnwald, Ermittelungen über Eingeborenenrechte der Südsee, *Zeitschrift für vergleichende Rechtswissenschaft*, XXXIII, p. 351.
[25] W. Gill, *Savage life in Polynesia* (1880), p. 120.

UNITY–DUALITY

L'Âme primitive (1927), pp. 250–1

In our eyes, an individual, however complex he may be, has the primordial and essential characteristic of being one. If he were not, he would no longer be an individual, he would be composed of many. But for primitive man, the living inner sense of his person is not so accompanied by a rigorous concept of individuality. Not only are its limits vague and imprecise, since the individual's appurtenances are part of him, and since his double, image, and reflection are part of him as well; further, the *tjurunga* of the Australian, the *kra* of the Ewe, the *ntoro* of the Ashanti, the 'namesake' of the Ba-ila, etc., without being entirely fused with the individual, are not distinguished from him either. Without this element, which establishes individuality by uniting it to the ancestors from whom it sprang, it could not exist. The individual is himself only on condition that he is at the same time other than himself. From this new point of view, far from being one, as we conceive it, the primitive is still one and many at the same time. Thus he is, so to speak, a real 'centre of participation'.

L'Âme primitive (1927), pp. 252–4

The 'duality' of the individual, in the representations of primitive men, seems to take two forms, and one might ask if it would not be better to study them separately. Sometimes the individual comprises what we judge to be two distinct beings, although for the primitive mentality it forms only one; such are the werewolf, the man-leopard, the sorcerer-crocodile, etc. Sometimes the duality is in fact a double presence. The same individual is found, at the same moment, in two places at once. One recalls the Indian who believed that Grubb had stolen some pumpkins from his garden although the latter was more than 200 kilometres away, or again the *baloyi* of Junod, and the *yoyova* sorcerers of Dr. Malinowski, who travel far to kill and eat their victims, all the while remaining in bed asleep at home. In all the examples of this second type, it seems less a question of duality than of the simultaneous presence of the same individual in two different places.

Nevertheless, this distinction, on close examination, is more apparent than real, and we have not thought it necessary to linger on it. More precisely, it exists only in our own mind, and the primitive mentality does not recognize it. For on the one hand, where we think we see a veritable duality, that is to say two distinct beings united in one by an intimate participation, it sees and feels this unity *first of all*, and it does not attach the same importance as we do to the fact that the two beings—the man and the leopard, for example—occupy different places in space. Thus, what we call duality is already a bi-presence for the primitive mentality, since in the man and the leopard it apprehends the same being straightaway. Inversely, what appears to us as a simple bi-presence is also a duality for it. If one says of the dreamer that his 'double' has gone far away and that it returns when the sleeper awakes, the primitive mentality will not object. It will admit that the witch who flies far away from her hut and the woman who remains in bed seem to be two people. In its eyes this duality, while very real, does not impede the fundamental unity of the individual. This lack of distinction between one and two, or even one and many, creates an intolerable difficult for our mind. At the very moment when it struggles to accept it, it instinctively repulses it, or else tries to resolve it by making it intelligible. The mind of primitive men, on the contrary, accepts it as it is and is satisfied. It is involved in their representations of the living, and we will find it again at the root of their representations of the dead.

L'Âme primitive (1927), pp. 328

In a large number of societies, if one wants to reach a dead man, who is remote and invisible, one acts on the corpse which remains. Consequently he is present and absent at one and the same time, or rather he is present in two—if not more—places at the same time. The corpse which one sees, and the deceased who has departed, are felt as forming but one and the same individual. There is abundant evidence on this point, and the only difficulty is that of which to choose.

L'Âme primitive (1927), pp. 339–40

In the eyes of primitive man, the dead man does not cease to exist. It is only his life on earth which has come to an end, and it continues elsewhere. The barrier between these two conditions is therefore not insurmountable; some living people may be represented as already dead, and some dead people as having come alive again. Nordenskiöld says very definitely: 'To die at one moment and to come alive again forthwith, is something which constantly happens in the stories of the Indians. This gives us a view of the representation which they make of death as consisting of a change of form. When one sleeps, one meets the dead; when one dies, one is sleeping for a long time. The survivors are never sure that the dead will not return. For the Indian, death is not a door through which it is impossible to retrace one's steps once one has passed through it.' [26]

This attitude is not restricted to the Indians of Bolivia, and in

[26] E. Nordenskiöld, *Forschungen und Abenteuer in Süd-Amerika* (1924), p. 297.

various regions many stories tell us of people who are dead and who have returned to life, and even of others, who, having every appearance of being still alive, are in fact dead. A sorcerer has killed them, and he considers it to his advantage to give them the appearance of life for a longer or shorter time. At first, nothing is changed in them, although he has deprived them of an essential appurtenance without which they will not be able to go on living for long, that is to say he has, according to the current expression, 'eaten their soul'. In fact, they are already dead, but those around them, and often they themselves do not perceive it. They are experiencing, so to speak, a delayed-action death.

THE MYSTICAL EXPERIENCE

L'Expérience mystique et les symboles chez les primitifs (1938), pp. 8–10

Taken as a whole, experience among primitive peoples is at the same time much poorer, and yet fuller than ours. For them it has been a starting-point leading to an ever wider knowledge of the facts and laws of nature. It has not allowed the applications of science which, in our civilizations, daily put more of the forces of nature to the service of man. It has not passed the stage of very scanty, although often very ingenious, empiricism. On the other hand, its domain is not limited to nature. Primitive men also feel themselves in immediate and constant touch with an invisible world which is no less real than the other; with their dead, recent or not, with 'spirits', with more or less clearly personified powers, and finally with the many types of beings which people their myths. It is to this experience that they owe a lot of data which they have no reason to reject as suspect: dreams, visions, omens, prodigies, warnings of every sort, etc. So many and so frequent are the contacts with the invisible world that they normally cause more emotion than surprise. These mystical experiences are thus imposed on primitive man with as much force as the others. They have no less influence on their behaviour. The idea of doubting this reality would not occur to them. Nothing incites them to reflect on them, and their every effort is to adapt themselves to them.

This being so, is there some objection to using the word

'experience' here, even though it concerns facts which, in our eyes, do not have the value of those which result from non-mystical experience, from verifiable and checkable experience? It does not seem so. Since, from the point of view of primitive men, mystical experience is in no way inferior to the other, it would not be a good method to approach the study by contesting its legitimacy. On the contrary, let us try to feel and think like them, really to adopt their attitude, and through an effort of empathy with them undergo their mystical experience.

One remark, however, is necessary. Our current notion of experience carries the stamp of certain mental habits belonging to the civilizations of the West. Since classical antiquity, it has been elaborated, over the course of centuries, by generations of philosophers, psychologists, logicians and learned men. Above all it has become, in their hands, a function of intelligence. Doubtless they have not under-estimated the presence of important affective elements, but it is not on these that their attention, from preference, has been centred. The essential role of experience, such as this tradition describes and analyses it, from Plato and his predecessors up to Kant and his successors, is to inform the thinking and the feeling subject about the properties of beings and objects with which it comes in contact, to make it perceive movements, impacts, sounds, colours, forms, smells, etc., and to allow the human mind, which reflects on these data and on their conditions, to create an image of the word for itself. The general notion of experience which is thus developed is above all 'cognitive'.

One cannot apply it just as it is to the experience of primitive peoples, which is above all 'affective'. Doubtless this latter also has as its function to teach them about the environment to which they have to adapt themselves at each instant, on pain of disappearing. This is the first condition of existence for humans, as for other living beings. Sometimes primitive peoples, in the most unfavourable climates, have managed to make marvellous use of the lessons of experience; the Eskimos in the arctic regions, the blackmen in the arid parts of Australia, and many others. Nevertheless, it is not only as a source of useful knowledge that their experience matters to them, but also insofar as it obtains for them facts of another sort which are of principal interest to them. Thereby, it is true, it adds almost nothing to their knowledge, but it discloses to them the presence and action of supernatural powers which surround them on every side, and on which, at every instant, their welfare and life depend.

It is not experience alone which teaches them of the existence of this invisible world; rather it confirms it. They are convinced of it in advance by tradition, and as we will show below it is very difficult to separate in such cases what is truly experience and what is belief. At the moment let us merely grasp that, among primitive peoples, a mystical experience is at one and the same time a revelation and a psychic complex where the affective elements occupy a preponderant place.

THE AFFECTIVE CATEGORY OF THE SUPERNATURAL

Le Surnaturel et la nature dans la mentalité primitive (1931), pp. xxxiv–xxxvi

Our traditional languages, grammars, philosophy, psychology and logic have accustomed us to consider generality as pertaining only to ideas. This generality appears in the operations which form the concepts, classify them, and establish their relationships. From this point of view, the understanding and assessment of generality belong to the intellect and to it alone. But in a differently directed mentality, not ruled as ours is by an Aristotelian, that is to say conceptual, ideal, and whose representations would often be of an essentially emotional nature, would not generality reside elsewhere than in ideas? In that case it would not really be 'known' but rather 'felt'. The general element would not consist of a constant factor, an object of intellectual perception, but rather in a coloration, or if one prefers it, a tonality common to certain representations, which the subject would immediately perceive as belonging to all of them.

In order to denote both the emotional nature and the generality of this element, which is furthermore inseparable from others in these representations, might one not say that they come under an *affective category*? 'Category' should not be taken either in the Aristotelian or Kantian sense, but merely as the uniting element in the mind for representations which, while differing from each other either in whole or part of their content, yet affect it in the same way. In other words, whatever may be the invisible power, or whatever the supernatural influence whose presence or action the primitive man suspects or perceives, the moment he is aware of it a wave of emotion, more or less strong, invades his consciousness. All representations of this type are similarly imbued. Each of them thus takes on a tonality which immediately re-immerses the subject in an affective state which he has already experienced many times. There is no need, therefore, for an intellectual effort to recognize it, for the affective category of the supernatural has come into play.

Such, it seems, is the underlying meaning in the many examples of primitive men telling us in various ways that 'The basis of our ideas concerning invisible powers is the fear which they inspire in us' or 'We do not believe, we fear.' What they wish to characterize thus is the fundamental and general element of their representations relative to the beings of the supernatural world. This element is not itself depicted in the proper sense of the word, but it is felt, and immediately recognized.

Undoubtedly we should enquire whether this affective category belongs exclusively to primitive mentality, or whether it does not rather correspond to a constant attitude of man in the presence of the supernatural. It is easier to discern among primitive peoples because of the frequent and considerable part which these emotional representations play in their life, but it is also found, although less distinctly, in other societies. Wherever the method of conceptual thought has developed and been prescribed, intellectual elements have taken an increasingly important place in the representations concerning the supernatural world. Then a flowering of beliefs has occurred, and often this has borne fruit in dogmas. But nevertheless the affective category of the supernatural survives, and the emotional basis of these representations is never entirely eliminated. Hidden, encapsulated, changed, it always remains recognizable. Every religion has known it. *Initium sapientiae timor Domini.*

THE UNUSUAL

L'Expérience mystique et les symboles chez les primitifs (1938), pp. 68–73

The impression made on primitive man by the appearance of or the encounter with something unusual is almost invariably the same. He is emotionally moved by it, sometimes thrown into confusion or stupefied; but surprise is rarely uppermost. Or, if one prefers it, it is a surprise for which his subconscious is prepared. He expects it without thinking. 'His attention is always on the alert; he is on the look-out for the unusual,' says Cailliet, speaking of the Malagasy.[27] The same observation has been made in regions widely separated from each other. Thus, in the Nicobar Islands, 'Anything that happens regularly is not supposed to require any cause, or at least one need not trouble about it. What happens only occasionally must have its cause, and the outward and visible circumstances which accompany the event can hardly be more than the instruments in the hands of unseen personalities. One must look beyond the phenomena to the real cause behind them, which in all probability will be found to be one of the innumerable spirits of land and sea and air.' [28]—'Again the mere strangeness or rarity of an object, . . . may give it [power].' [29]

In South Africa, one of the first missionaries to see the Bechuana made the following observation, 'Everything in a state of ignorance, which is not known, and which is involved in

[27] E. Cailliet, *Symbolisme et âmes primitives* (1936), p. 72.
[28] G. Whitehead, *In the Nicobar Islands* (1924), p. 147.
[29] F. E. Williams, *Papuans of the Trans-Fly* (1936), p. 323

mystery, is the object of superstitious veneration, where second causes are unknown, and invisible agency is substituted in their places.'[30] Among the Dinka (of the Anglo–Egyptian Sudan), '. . . there is no happening or event however little out of the common that is not regarded as of religious significance and as an occasion for sacrifice. . . . As a concrete example we may cite the behaviour, as related to us by the Rev. H. Lea Wilson, of a Cic Dinka who noticed an unusually large pumpkin in his garden. The vegetable was not cut; on the contrary the owner, saying . . . 'the spirit has fallen', prepared to sacrifice a goat . . . and the blood [was] allowed to run over the vegetable. . . . When aeroplanes first appeared . . . some fifty bulls were slaughtered, while one old man confessed to a murder committed several years before.'[31]

The terms employed to express the impression made on primitive man by the appearance of or an encounter with the unusual are thus almost everywhere the same: mystery, superstitious veneration, divine origin, religious meaning, warning of divinities, etc. Obviously, this encounter acts on them as an unexpected and dangerous contact with the invisible powers, and their reaction has almost the uniformity of a reflex.

How is it that this mystical experience is thus invariably accompanied by a characteristic emotion about which they have no doubts, and where the elements of fear predominate? 'Accompanied' is an understatement, for this emotion is an integral and essential part of the experience itself. Why this apparently instinctive dread of contact with the supernatural powers? They are not all regarded as hostile by definition, nor always maleficent, and in certain circumstances primitive men spare no effort to ensure the presence and support of some of them. Let us briefly recall the initiation and fertility ceremonies which hold such a place in the life of the Australians, Papuans, and Melanesians, where they seek to obtain a participation, a communion with

[30] J. Philip, *Researches in South Africa*, II (1828), pp. 116–17.

[31] C. G. & B. Z. Seligman, *Pagan tribes of the Nilotic Sudan* (1932), p. 178.

certain of their dead, of their mythic heroes, and of their totemic ancestors; the efforts of young North American Indians to be worthy that a spirit should come and award them the favour of a vision and a revelation, and finally the custom so widespread, as we will see below, of inducing dreams in which one will receive the advice of invisible beings, etc.

Thus, what is feared is not the contact with them itself, but their assumed disposition. Above all it is the unusual nature either of the being or object which appears, or of the encounter which, by revealing its presence, immediately puts into action the affective category of the supernatural. This is an emotion similar to that which accidents provoke. The latter, as we saw in the last chapter, are immediately sensed and interpreted not simply as misfortunes, but also, and above all, as ill-omens, such as were the *monstra* and *portenta* of the Romans.

This quasi-religious fear inspired by the unusual is often expressed in a striking fashion by proverbs. Here are some typical examples: 'What has brought what does not usually come, is to see what is not normally seen.' This is to say, as Gaden explains, that every unusual event has some equally unexpected consequences. 'He who sees something he does not recognize should not wait for someone to shout "flee".' That is to say: One must run away as fast as possible from every unusual thing. 'Whatever does not usually die, if it is dead, those who skin it will be frightened to do so.' That is to say: whatever does not usually die is an animal unknown in that place or a monster, and one touches it only with fear, for everything unusual is frightening, and should be distrusted. It is said to express the fear inspired by a thing which is not normally seen.[32]

The unusual nature of a being, object or encounter thus reveals the presence of powers whose action will be baleful. It is not so much because they are mysterious and unknown that they cause fear, but, on the contrary, it is because one knows that in appearing in this fashion they certainly presage a misfortune, without

[32] H. Gaden, 'Proverbes et maximes Peuls et Toucouleurs', *Travaux et mémoires de L'Institut d'ethnologie*, XVI, pp. 283–4.

however making known what it will be. The threat is only the graver for this.

The primitive mentality, as we know, distinguishes poorly between 'portentous sign' and 'cause'. Omens are not simple pieces of information about what is going to happen, nor even simple warnings concerning what should be avoided or done. They have their own effectiveness, and help to bring about what they predict. Thus if the unusual announces misfortune by its appearance, it is also partly responsible for the dire consequences which will certainly follow. In this way, strange and extraordinary events and beings, which are out of the common and infringe the customary rules, are already harmful by the mere fact of their appearance. They do not solely reveal that a harmful action is going to happen thereafter. They themselves are already bringing it about.

MYTHS AND LEGENDS

La Mythologie primitive (1935), pp. vii–ix

In general, the 'primitive' myths which we have at our disposal are fragmentary and incomplete. Only a small number of people in a tribe possess a wide knowledge of them. This knowledge is the privilege of old men, who, having passed the successive stages of initiation, are married and have children. Each of them knows a greater or smaller number, but often does not know either the beginning or the end, or is ignorant of important parts of it. It is rare that one can obtain an entire myth from a single informant.

Further, the myths of a given tribe, with certain exceptions, hardly form a whole. It has often been noticed that they remain independent of and as it were indifferent to each other. The mythology of a tribe may be of inexhaustible richness without appearing to have any unifying factor. Landtman has found this characteristic very marked in the mythology of the Papuans of Kiwai Island.[33] It is not what we would have expected, yet doubtless our surprise arises from the earlier speculations on mythology which, unknown to us, still remain in our mind. In the 18th and 19th centuries people sought in mythology, and naturally found, a concerted effort to account for the origin of things, analogous, in an older form, to the similar effort of theology and metaphysics. In fact, this philosophy of myth scarcely related to any-

[33] G. Landtman, *The Kiwai Papuans of British New Guinea* (1927), pp. 298–9.

thing other than contemporary mythologies of already developed religions, or of metaphysical doctrines whose influence they revealed. Faced with myths such as those from Australia or New Guinea, these theorists could not have failed to recognize the lack of coordination.

This trait is not peculiar to the Australian and Papuan mythologies. It has also been reported in those of other societies whose civilization is more or less on the same rung of the ladder. To cite only one example, from the Andaman Islands, 'One feature of the legends that must be pointed out is their unsystematic nature. The same informant may give, on different occasions, two entirely different versions of such a thing as the origin of fire, or the beginning of the human race. The Andamanese, to all appearance, regard each little story as independent, and do not consciously compare one with another. They thus seem to be entirely unconscious of what are obvious contradictions to the student of the legends.' [34]

La Mythologie primitive (1935), pp. 45–6

A number of Australian and Papuan myths relate the adventures and valiant deeds of 'ancestors' and 'culture heroes'. Endowed with extraordinary powers, they have produced, 'created', everything which the real world contains: living species, inanimate objects, and the salient features of the region (lakes, rivers, mountains, rocks, etc.). They are also the founders of institutions, and the authors of the essential inventions which have made social life possible. At the same time, they had the faculty of taking at their own will any form which pleased them.

Now, almost always (the exceptions are rare), the myths represent these ancestors or culture heroes as being at one and the same time human and animal. On this point, the evidence is abundant and unanimous. Spencer and Gillen never tire of saying it and repeating it about the tribes of Central Australia. In the

[34] A. R. Radcliffe-Brown, *The Andaman islanders* (1922), p. 188.

myths and the ceremonial texts collected by Strehlow, it is a *leitmotiv*. Among the Marind-anim, the *Dema* appear sometimes in human form, and sometimes in another, either animal or vegetable; they change from one to the other with great ease.

This characteristic of mythical persons, constant in Australia and New Guinea among the tribes which we will consider here more especially, is also recorded among their neighbours, and, it is true to say, among primitive societies in general. Ehrenreich has pointed it out in the oldest myths of South American Indians, and it no less frequent in those of the North American Indians, particularly among the Plains Indians and those of the North-west Coast (British Columbia). It appears with the same regularity in the myths of black Africa. In brief, it does not seem bound up with the social structure of the Australian and Papuan tribes (which moreover is far from presenting a uniform type among all of them), nor dependent on any local condition. Almost everywhere that myths of this type have been collected, the ancestors and culture heroes which they mention appear at one and the same time in human and animal form.

La Mythologie primitive (1935), pp. 316–19

'Folk tales' care little about the logical or physical possibility of the marvels which they relate, and hardly more for the psychological probability. In the fairy stories which we were recalling just now, a cat who is also a man becomes a great lord without ceasing to be a cat. In less time than it takes to write it, a pumpkin is turned into a coach, and a large rat into a coachman. Here we are in a world as fluid as that of the myths of Australia and New Guinea, and no less incompatible with the laws of nature and the logical requirements of our thought. However, we do not turn away from these stories as being childish, pointless or grotesque fabrications. Why is it that, on the contrary, we find our interest in them constantly renewed?

The persistence of this taste will appear less strange if we remember that, since time immemorial, these stories have been spread from one end of the world to the other, and have almost always been considered, with certain exceptions, as 'true histories', at least by primitive peoples who lack the sense of impossibility. There, those who transmit them have accepted them as such from their parents, and the young who hear them do as much in their turn, with no more difficulty. If we could go back far enough into the past, we should doubtless see that our own ancestors were no exception on this point. Thus, in fact, what needs explaining is not why in so many more or less primitive societies people believe, in all simplicity, in the truth of the majority of these stories, but on the contrary, why, in our own society, we ceased to believe them a long time ago.

Without doubt, the reason for it lies, at least partly, in the rational character of the civilization which classical antiquity established and bequeathed to us. Uncheckable and unverifiable data, that is to say, those data derived from the mystical experience through which the action of invisible and supernatural agents is revealed, have been gradually excluded from experience accepted as valid. In other words, the domain of reality tended, more and more exactly, to coincide with that of the laws of nature and of thought. Anything outside these boundaries would henceforth be rejected as impossible (true religious experience excepted). This is to say that, for minds which have oriented themselves in this way and which have thus broken with the primitive mentality, the mythical world, and the world of folklore which is not truly distinct from it, could no longer form part of reality.

However, history shows that this mental foundation is far from common. It has been established in only a few societies, and has cost them centuries of effort. Even there, it is far short of being universal or constant. What does this mean, if not that it requires a strict discipline, and that the human mind, if it obeys its originally dominant tendencies, is scarcely aware of the impossibilities of the mythical world, and does not consider excluding the data of mystical experience from the realm of reality?

Thus this exclusion, although rational, or rather because

rational, entails, even where it is habitual, a constraint, and, according to current usage, an inhibition. These tendencies, left to themselves, would push the mind in a very different direction. To resist them without weakening, it must watch its smallest steps, and constantly do itself a sort of violence.

Here lies the underlying reason for the charm which draws us towards folk tales, and the seductiveness of their language. As soon as we listen, this constraint is suspended, this violence ceases. In a moment, in a single leap, the repressed tendencies regain the lost ground. When we hear these stories, we voluptuously abandon the rational attitude, we no longer submit to its demands. We are not unaware that we will soon have to take it up again, nor even that we are not leaving it for good; if it were in earnest, we would look twice. But such as it is, this relaxation, while it lasts, pleases our innermost being. We feel ourselves becoming again similar to the men who formerly (as still today in so many areas) considered the mystical part of their experience to be as real, or even more so, as the positive part. It is more than a recreation, it is a relaxation. The enjoyment which it gives us goes far beyond simple amusement.

This explains how folk tales cross civilizations and centuries almost intact. On us, in particular, the attraction which they exert is always new, and runs no risk of becoming weaker. As if by a wave of the wand which their fairies use so freely, we are abruptly transported back to the ancestral attitude. We then see the mysterious and fluid world of the oldest myths live again before our eyes. Far though we believe ourselves to be from the mentality which produced them, this spectacle captivates and holds us,

> 'And I myself, while moralizing too,
> If I the tale of the Ass-skin should hear,
> I'd listen to it with a well pleas'd ear.[35]

[35] [Translator's note.] *La Fontaine's Fables*. Translated by Robert Thomson (Paris, 1806). Book VIII, Fable iv, p. 50.

RITUAL CEREMONIES

Le Surnaturel et la nature dans la mentalité primitive (1931)
pp. 110–13

We are used, at least in the West, to seeing the religious feeling of dependence and the need for protection and communion accompanied by the representation of one or many superior beings. It is from them or him that one implores help and succour, and it is from them or him that one hopes for salvation. We barely conceive of worship without more or less clearly defined and personalized deities. Now, in a large number of primitive tribes, we find no such thing. '. . . their performance [of ceremonies]' write Spencer and Gillen, 'is not associated in the native mind with the idea of appealing to the assistance of any supernatural being.'[36] Assuredly, Spencer and Gillen do not mean to contest that the Arunta, in their ceremonies, are seeking to obtain the assistance of mystical agencies. On the contrary, this is, according to them, their principal reason for existing. But they have never observed in any of them that the natives had in mind an individual being such as a deity, devil, or spirit.

Without doubt it is difficult for us to understand very complicated practices of a propitiatory nature, the result of which has to take place magically and, so to speak, automatically, without addressing a being capable of understanding, capable of being persuaded, appeased, touched, etc. Nevertheless this is how many

[36] Spencer & Gillen, *The Native Tribes of Central Australia* (1899), p. 170.

primitive people carry on, and the previous chapters allow us to see the reason. Primitive peoples consider the dispositions of beings, whatever they may be, not as tendencies or states of an essentially psychic nature, but as semi-physical realities on which one can act directly by magical means. There is thus no need for them to imagine the invisible beings which they seek to conciliate as individual beings, and still less as people, although they sometimes do so.

As to the elements peculiar to these ceremonies, which are not met or which are scarcely recognizable in the worship of other societies, a brief analysis of the facts will make them apparent. This analysis will at the same time attempt to determine, as far as possible, what the essential features of these ceremonies mean.

In the first place, they almost always include, in Australia, New Guinea, and elsewhere as well, some kind of dramatic representations. Actors are appointed (according to the clans especially concerned in each episode of the ceremony), and each entrusted with a role which has to be carefully learned and rehearsed. The dance-measure is given by the women, who clap their hands or slap their thighs rhythmically; often also they use drums. Finally the audience, which follows with enthusiasm the scenes whose ins and outs it knows in advance, is made up of the rest of the tribe, and of neighbouring tribes if guests have come from these.

The dances which the Plains Indians of North America used to perform before going on a buffalo hunt have often been described, as, for example, by Catlin and Maximilian von Neuwied. In them the Indians used to represent and to 'act' the events of the hunt. One of them, covered in a buffalo hide, imitated the movements of the animal at pasture; others, the hunters, approached him with infinite care, and attacked him without a moment's warning, etc. But one must go beyond this charade since this is only the ceremony seen from outside. It has also a deep symbolic sense. In reality, it is anything but a game. In the Indians' thought, it acts mystically on the behaviour of the buffalo, and its effectiveness is such that they will let themselves be seen, approached and killed. So too, in certain episodes of the initiation ceremonies among the Arunta, 'At the first glance it looks much as if all that they were intended to represent was the behaviour of certain animals, but in reality they have a much deeper meaning, for each performer represents an ancestral individual who lived in [the mystic age of] the Alcheringa [hence a totemic animal].' [37]

Here is not the place to analyse and interpret in detail the ceremonies described by Spencer and Gillen, some of which last several months. We will recall only that in them everything has a mystical meaning, from the first moment of 'singing the ground' on which the ceremony will take place and when the young men draw blood from a vein in the arm which spurts over the other actors, until the moment when the ceremony closes with the destruction of the objects used in it.

Most frequently there is no single end pursued. By imitating what, in certain circumstances, the mythical ancestors have done, and by reproducing their gestures and actions, one has communion with them and truly shares in their essence. At the same time, the novices, the young generation which is going to join its forerunners, are introduced to the secret of the sacred rites upon which the well-being and salvation of the group periodically depend. Moreover, at the same time, by virtue of the ceremonies, one is able to multiply, to make grow and increase the totemic plants and animals of the various clans of the tribe.

Le Surnaturel et la nature dans la mentalité primitive (1931), pp. 124–5

The natives do not only count upon the magical quality belonging to the rites, dances, songs, etc., but they also base their hopes on the help of ancestors or the recently deceased whose presence the ceremonies ensure. Observers whose material is detailed

[37] Spencer & Gillen, *The Native Tribes of Central Australia* (1899), p. 228.

enough nearly always make express mention of this. But even if they had not mentioned it, we would have been justified in making up for their silence if they told us that use is made of masks other than those of animals in the ceremonies and dances concerned. For there appears no doubt that, in almost all dances, the wearers of these masks represent 'spirits', that is to say, with some exceptions, of the dead or of ancestors.

Now, 'represent' here ought to be understood in its literal etymological sense which is how primitive people would take the word if they used it: *to make present again*, or *to make reappear what has disappeared*. As long as the actors and the dancers wear these masks, and from the sole fact that the masks are on them, they are not solely the representatives of the dead and the ancestors whom the masks portray, but for a time they effectively become and really *are* these dead and these ancestors. In the eyes of primitive peoples, as one knows, there is nothing inconceivable or even shocking about the bi-presence; accordingly the inhabitants of the other world can, without leaving it, appear in this one, if one knows how to recall them. This is exactly the virtue of the ceremony.

To wear a mask, therefore, is something very different from a game. It is among the most serious and weighty acts in the world: a direct and immediate contact, and even an intimate participation, with the beings of the invisible world, from whom one expects vital favours. The individuality of the actor gives place momentarily to that of the 'spirit' which he represents, or rather they are fused together.

THE TERM 'PRELOGICAL' ABANDONED IN THE POSTHUMOUS *CARNETS*

Les Carnets (1949), pp. 129–30

The step which I have just taken, and hope is decisive, consists, in a word, in abandoning a badly posed problem, which resulted in some inextricable difficulties, and in confining myself to a question the terms of which are suggested by the facts alone. Until now, I had not entirely renounced the assumptions [Voraussetzungen] fixed in my mind at the time of writing *Les Fonctions mentales* and which dominated its composition. There is no doubt that for some time I have not spoken of a logic other than our own, nor used the term 'prelogical', and have given up speaking of the law of participation. But the very essence of this idea exists without this form; participation still seemed to me to be something essential to the primitive mentality, and probably to the human mind, making a complement and perhaps a counterweight to the regulating principles of logical thought. But if this is so, where does participation's field of action begin and end? How can one understand that it might be something essential to the structure of the human mind, which necessarily intervenes in the representation which the mind forms of objects and beings, and whose function has had to wait until the 20th century to be recorded? That neither psychologists, nor logicians, nor even metaphysicans such as Plato and Malebranche, who have spoken, and excellently, on certain participations, have attributed to it the function in the mind which was recognized in *Les Fonctions mentales*? And, since it seems that participation involves something deeply rebellious to intelligibility, how is one to understand that the human mind could be at one and the same time the mainspring of the rational and irrational?

From this it follows that, even allowing for the numerous and characteristic cases of participation of which my six volumes are full, there still exist doubts about the explanation—even as modestly reduced in Volumes 5 and 6[38]—I have given of them in invoking the presence of mental habits different from ours among 'primitive peoples'. But, even with these conclusions, I still want to account for participation, if not from the logical point of view, at least from the viewpoint of the knowledge of objects, and of their understanding—while recognizing that this understanding, when it concerns participations, entails an important part of affective, not cognitive, elements.

Les Carnets (1949), pp. 131–2

If I glance over all I have written on the subject of participation between 1910 and 1938, the development of my ideas seems clear to me. I started by positing a primitive mentality different from ours, if not in its structure at least in its function, and I found myself in difficulties in explaining the relationships of this mentality with the other, not only among us but also among primitive peoples. In short, I had only juxtaposed them, without being able to account for either their coexistence or their relations. A position which I have never been able to defend well, and in the long run an untenable one. By limiting myself to discussing mental customs, I took refuge in withdrawal. But the thesis thus extenuated and weakened is no more defensible. One will then ask whence these customs arise, and how, in themselves, they constitute a 'mentality' which, in an inexplicable fashion, coexists with the logical exercise of our mental activity.

[38] I.e., *La Mythologie primitive* and *L'Expérience mystique*. [Editor's note.]

Let us then give up this retreat in its turn and without a backward thought, that is to say, let us entirely give up explaining participation by something peculiar to the human mind, either constitutional (in its structure or function) or acquired (mental customs). In other words, let us expressly rectify what I believed correct in 1910: there is not a primitive mentality distinguishable from the other by *two* characteristics which are peculiar to it (mystical and prelogical). There is a mystical mentality which is more marked and more easily observable among 'primitive peoples' than in our societies, but it is present in every human mind. From the moment that it is no longer set up as something which is opposed to a different mentality, all the above problems disappear.

Once the obstructing hypotheses have been brushed aside, we no longer have to ask ourselves: 'What is this participation which the primitive mentality (or the human mind) feels and apprehends between objects and beings? Why does it feel it on such an occasion and not on another?' We put ourselves simply on the level of facts. Let us study in what circumstances and under what conditions, primitive peoples (and we ourselves) feel and represent participations. Perhaps the very simple reason why, in other circumstances and under other conditions, participation has no role to play will emerge directly from this study.

FURTHER READING

Allusions to the theory of Lévy-Bruhl can be found in a large number of books. Consequently the list below cannot be presented as exhaustive.

Lenoir, R. 'La mentalité primitive' (*Revue de métaphysique et de morale*, 1922, pp. 199–224. A critical study of *La Mentalité primitive*).

Blondel, Charles. *La Mentalité primitive* (Stock, 1926), A very clear résumé of the first two books devoted by Lévy-Bruhl to this subject.

Larguier des Bancels, Jean. 'Prélogique et civilisés' (*Archives de psychologie*, Geneva, May 1926, pp. 1–12).

Allier, Raoul. *Le non-civilisé et nous* (Irreducible difference or fundamental identity?) (Payot, 1927). A critical study of Lévy-Bruhl's theories about primitive peoples.

Leroy, Olivier. *La Raison primitive* (*Essai de réfutation de la théories du prélogisme*) (Geuthner, 1927).

Essertier, Daniel. *Les formes inférieures de l'explication* (Alcan, 1927). Statement of a theory which is different from that of Lévy-Bruhl but which, on certain points, is inspired by it.

Van der Leeuw, G. *La Structure de la mentalité primitive* (An extract from the *Revue d'histoire et de philosophie religieuse*, Alcan, Strasbourg, 1928). A study based on the works of Lévy-Bruhl and psychopathology.

Bergson, Henri. *Les deux sources de la morale et de la religion* (Alcan, 1932). A discussion of Lévy-Bruhl's theory (cf. in particular, pp. 150 ff.).

Davy, Georges. *Sociologues d'hier et d'aujourd'hui* (1st ed., 1931; 2nd ed. revised and enlarged, P.U.F., 1950). The whole of the fourth part of this work is a detailed account and a penetrating examination of Lévy-Brulh's sociology. The last chapter of the 2nd edition gives a general view of the character and work of Lévy-Bruhl.

Aldrich, C. R. *The Primitive Mind and Modern Civilization* (Kegan Paul, London, 1931). This study, made from a Jungian point of view, is partly inspired by the works of Lévy-Bruhl.

Ouy, Achille. 'La mentalité primitive chez les peuples civilisés' (in *Mélanges économiques et sociaux offerts à Émile Witmeur*, Libraire du Recueil Sirey, Paris, 1939, pp. 264–70).

Przyluski, Jean. *La Participation* (P.U.F., 1940). See particularly the Introduction.

Van der Leeuw, G. *L'Homme primitif et la religion* (P.U.F., 1940). Revival of certain themes treated by Lévy-Bruhl, but from a phenomenological viewpoint.

Gurvitch, Georges. *Morale théorique et science des moeurs* (P.U.F., 1st ed. 1948; 3rd ed. revised and corrected, 1961). In the first chapter of this work will be found an account of Lévy-Bruhl's *La Morale et la science de moeurs*, followed by a critical examination of it.

Bréhier, Émile. 'Originalité de Lévy-Bruhl' (in the *Revue philosophique*, October–December, 1949, pp. 385–8).

Bastide, Roger. 'Contribution à l'étude de la participation' (in *Cahiers internationaux de Sociologie*, Vol. XIV, 1953, pp. 30–40).

Revue philosophique October–December 1957. (This is a special issue devoted to the centenary of Lévy-Bruhl's birth, and contains numerous articles on this author and his work).

Charevskaia, B. 'Confusions méthodologiques et terminologiques dans la question de mentalité des primitifs' (in *Sovietskaia ethnografia*, 1958, No. 6, pp. 61–75. A critical examination of Lévy-Bruhl's theories from a Marxist point of view).

Gurvitch, Georges. *Traité de sociologie* (P.U.F., Vol. I, 1958, pp. 52–4; Vol. II, pp. 107–9).

Gilson, Étienne. *Le Philosophe et la théologie* (A. Fayard, 1960), pp. 34, 35, 38, 43, 98 and 107.

Cazeneuve, Jean. *La Mentalité archaïque* (A. Colin, 1961). A résumé of each of Lévy-Bruhl's works on primitive peoples, pp. 7–45).